AF413247

Evolved

Evolved

From the Fields of Farm Labor
to the United States Department of Labor

CEOLA WALKER COLES

A Memoir

Scripture Quotations: By King James Version of the Bible

Inspiration Page Quote:
"When you've worked hard, and done well, and walked through that doorway of opportunity… you do not slam it shut behind you … you reach back, and you give other folks the same chances that helped you succeed." — Michelle Obama

Song Title: "If I can help somebody, my living shall not be in vain." By Mahalia Jackson

Cover Design:
Ceola Walker Coles
Butterfly image created by Microsoft Bing Copilot

Author Cover Photo by:
Original Photo: Theresa Knox Photography
Editing and Color Background Modification: Cameras, Etc., Newark, DE

Photos by:
Ceola Walker Coles
Carnival Cruise Line

ISBN: 979-8-3481-2484-7

DEDICATION

To all those who have embarked on the challenging path of self-improvement and professional growth, this memoir is dedicated to you. I hope it will serve as a beacon of hope and inspiration towards a fulfilling and rewarding work life. Your ambition, perseverance, and adaptability are the keys to success.

This memoir is a story that honors the human capacity to overcome, to grow, and to thrive against all odds. This memoir is my legacy, and every word I write is a testament to my life's journey. It may be a testament to your journey for walking a similar path to transform your work life. I hope this memoir will be a blessing to you and inspire you to find your own resilience and to embrace the journey that lies ahead.

INTRODUCTION

Evolved: From the Fields of Farm Labor to the United States Department of Labor is a testament to the power of resilience, hard work, and determination. My journey began in the humble fields where my siblings and I toiled sun up to sun down, learning the values of responsibility and work ethics from a young age. We worked alongside our parents, contributing to the family's livelihood, despite the challenges of living in a dysfunctional home filled with fear, physical and emotional abuse, and drama.

The turning point came when my mother and I left home, escaping the cruel environment that threatened to stifle our spirits. We moved in secrecy, unable to inform family or friends of our whereabouts for fear of being found and forced to return. This period of our lives was marked by uncertainty and hardship, but it also forged a deep sense of resilience within me.

Growing up, I juggled full-time and part-time jobs to ensure a better quality of life. Each job I held was a stepping-stone leading me closer to my true calling. From earning fifty cents for a basket of beans to working for a dollar an hour, I eventually found a professional career within the United States Department of Labor. There I dedicated myself to helping people and earned a six-figure salary. The true measure of my success is the impact I made *and* the person I became.

This memoir is a reflection of my evolution, from the fields of farm labor to a respected, professional position within the federal government.

It is a story of overcoming adversity, embracing opportunities, and finding purpose in service to others. I hope my journey inspires you to believe in the power of prayer, perseverance, and the possibility of transformation, no matter where you start.

INSPIRATION

"When you've worked hard, and done well, and walked through that doorway of opportunity ... you do not slam it shut behind you ... you reach back, and you give other folks the same chances that helped you succeed."

— Michelle Obama

This quote from Michelle Obama perfectly captures the essence of my journey and the values I hold dear. From the fields of farm labor to the U.S. Department of Labor, my path has been marked by resilience, hard work, and determination.

I have faced many challenges, but each step forward was made possible by the opportunities I seized and the support I received from those who believed in me. This spirit of giving back and lifting others is what drives me to share my story.

Through this memoir, I hope to inspire others facing their own struggles. May it serve as a reminder that with hard work and determination, you can achieve your dreams. Once you do, remember to reach back and help others along the way.

ACKNOWLEDGEMENTS

As I embark on this journey through the pages of my life, I am filled with gratitude. I don't forget where I come from or who helped to get me where I am. First, giving honor to God, from whom all my blessings flow, and then to those who have been a positive influence in my life:

- To my mother, Gladys Walker, whose love and sacrifices laid my foundation, and who encouraged me to do better with my life. Although she is no longer with me, her prayers continue to bless me, and her sweet spirit watches over me and guides me along the way.

- To my Aunts who supported my mother and me during the most difficult times of my journey: Hazel Calderon provided shelter and nourishment, and shared her wisdom and guidance which contributed to my personal and career development. Mary (Doll) Brooks was instrumental in helping my mother and I start a new life, and she encouraged me, with her inspiring letters and uplifting scriptures, to never give up on my goals. Mable Dale provided shelter and nourishment when we needed it most. Betty Watford's prayers over the phone gave me health and strength when I didn't think I would make it. And Betty Walker recommended various job search locations and taught me to "Think Big."

- To my dearest friends: Louise, Gwen, and Roslyn. My childhood friend, Louise, encouraged me to write about my work and life experiences for a "Prior Learning Portfolio" to gain college credits, and that led me to write my memoir. Gwen inspired me to go back to college and get my degree. And Roslyn offered insights on how to handle challenging college courses. Each of my friends are very special to me.

- To my supervisors, who gave me an opportunity, colleagues who encouraged me, and to the strangers who guided me in the right direction.

- **To my beloved husband, my rock.** You were always there for me as I ventured out to develop new skills. Your support and encouragement empowered me to follow my dreams and achieve my goals.

CONTENTS

HUMBLE BEGINNINGS: ROOTS OF RESILIENCE

They say you can't know where you're going until you know where you've been, and don't forget where you come from, you may have to go back again. My story unfolds growing up and working on various farms in South Jersey where the values of hard work and perseverance were planted deep within me long before I stepped foot into the halls of the United States Department of Labor.

On January 27, 1951, I was born in Bridgeton, New Jersey — a small rural town — to my mother, Gladys Walker, and my father, Robert Walker. I am the fourth of six children — three brothers and two sisters. Most of my family have passed away. My youngest sister, Geraldine, was an infant when she passed in the early 1950s. My father was tragically robbed and stabbed to death in his home in 1978. My mother passed peacefully in her sleep on Christmas Eve, December 1989, from congestive heart failure. My youngest brother, Morris, reportedly died by suicide in January 1991. My oldest brother, Bobby, passed in June 2006 from lung cancer, and my middle brother, Charlie (CT), passed in September 2023 from throat and lung cancer. Now, two of us are left: my older sister, Joyce Jeanette, and me.

My parents were economically disadvantaged. My father, born to a poor family in Augusta, Georgia, was the oldest of 15 children and had only a third-grade education. My mother, also born to a poor family in Winston-Salem, North Carolina, was the eldest of 11 children and had a seventh-grade education. In their generation, farm work took precedence over education. As long as they could write their names and count money that was deemed sufficient.

The house I grew up in was not built by professionals. My father and a neighbor with some carpentry knowledge constructed our small two-bedroom bungalow. In the 1950s, I remember our house lacked plumbing, air conditioning, heating, and an inside bathroom. We had an outside toilet, a water pump in the kitchen, a large kerosene stove in the living room near my parents' room (it heated the living room and also their room), and a small oil stove in our bedroom. By early morning, the fire would go out, and the room was so cold you could see your breath.

Our bedroom had two beds for the five of us kids. My sister and I shared one bed, while my three brothers shared the other. The bedrooms had no built-in closets; we hung our clothes on wire hangers placed on large nails behind the doors. My parents had an old second-hand cedar wardrobe closet in their room. My mother had more clothes than my father, including pretty hats and dresses for church and parties. My father, a truck driver, had several tan uniforms, one dark blue suit, and a few casual shirts and pants.

In the early 1960s, my parents installed a bathroom. I learned that it was a county requirement for residents on our street. Our sky-blue bathroom was a welcome change. No more outside toilet or "night pot." I cherished our new bathroom and loved decorating it with Mom's pretty towels. This passion for beautiful towel arrangements and decorating has stayed with me.

The back of our house was surrounded by woods. Back then, having woods behind your house signified poverty. Today, a wooded lot is considered prime property for privacy. My parents raised pigs and chickens, and our wooded lot hid the pigpen and chicken coop from neighbors in the back of our house. We had a small vegetable garden of corn, cucumbers, tomatoes, and collard greens. These were our main food sources. On "hog killing day," neighbors helped with the slaughtering and cleaning process. We had plenty of bacon, pork sausage, pork chops, ham, pig feet, and chitterlings. We ate so much pork and chicken that now I cannot stand it. I prefer only seafood.

The woods also brought large rats that chewed their way into our house. My parents set traps, but they were too small. Even our cat couldn't handle them. Finally, our dog Tiny took care of them. It was a relief when they were gone.

We didn't realize how poor we were until one winter day when my parents, siblings, and I were behind a grocery store taking expired food from the trash bins. We found dairy products, meats, and canned goods — foods my parents couldn't afford to buy. Despite our poverty, we always had a roof over our heads, clothes on our backs, clean beds to sleep in, and food on the table. We were never hungry. Both parents cooked. Mom cooked most of the time. We had a full course meal, dessert, and Kool-Aid on Sundays. After changing our Sunday church clothes, we looked forward to Sunday dinner, a tradition I still cherish … except for the Kool-Aid.

My mother often shopped at thrift stores for our clothes and household items. She couldn't always afford new clothes from regular stores, but she washed and cleaned everything before we wore them. To this day, I refuse to shop in thrift stores because it reminds me of when my parents couldn't do better. Now I can.

On special occasions, like Easter and back-to-school, my parents bought us brand new clothes. I recall a children's clothing store downtown called Mays, where Mom bought my sister and me pretty nylon dresses and patent leather shoes for church. Working in the fields during the summer brought extra money for new school clothes and shoes. When our school shoes had holes from walking a mile to our school on a dirt road, we put cardboard inside to cover the holes. It lasted until it rained. Eventually, my parents bought us black and white Buster Brown shoes with rubber soles, and my brothers wore Brogan shoes. We hated these shoes. They took forever to wear out!

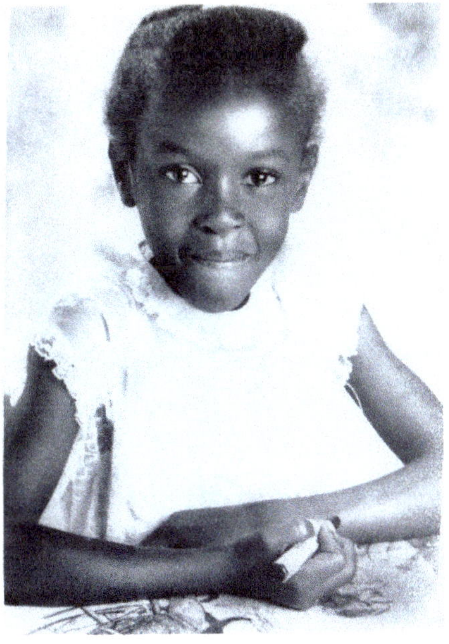

Life's journey is a mosaic of experiences — each piece a testament to the lessons learned and the growth achieved. As a child, I learned that responsibility was not just a word, but a way of life. It was in the simplicity of caring for my toddler brother, in the trust placed upon me by my parents, and in the lessons learned from following instructions with diligence and commitment. Responsibility taught me reliability at a very young age. These early experiences laid the foundation for the beginning of my work life.

At five years old, when I was in kindergarten, I attended school for just a half day until noon. My older siblings were in higher grades — 2nd, 4th, and 6th — and stayed in school until around 3:00 p.m. By the time they arrived home after walking about a mile, it would have been too late for Mom to leave for work. So, it was my responsibility to take care of my baby brother.

When I would come home from school, Mom would explain that my baby brother was already cleaned, fed, and asleep in bed. Her instructions were to watch him until my older siblings came home from school. If he cried, I was to give him a bottle and pat him back to sleep. Mom had the bottle of milk already prepared in his bed. Sometimes, I had to decide if it was necessary to take him out of bed, hold him and give him his bottle, because he didn't always go back to sleep with just a few pats, especially when I sensed he was crying for Mom.

After Mom gave me my lunch, I would lay down on the bed next to my brother's bed in my parent's room and take my nap. I would be home alone for about three hours after Mom left to do domestic work. Her further instructions were to stay in the house until my siblings (ages 7, 9, and 12) came home from school. We were never concerned about someone breaking in or bothering us.

In the 1950s, people respected each other's property, and everyone knew each other in our neighborhood. We had family next door and friends across the street if we needed anything.

When Mom's schedule changed to early mornings, I had to miss several days of school. As a result, my teacher, Mrs. Valentine, explained that because I had missed too many days, I had to repeat kindergarten. However, since I was so far ahead of my classmates, my teacher promoted me to the first grade after just a few weeks.

In today's society, what I was responsible for would be considered child neglect or abuse, and parents would be jailed for leaving a five-year-old child home alone with a two-year-old toddler. In the 1950s, this was the way of life for most families, especially poor ones. There was no such thing as hiring a babysitter; the oldest child was responsible for taking care of the youngest.

Sometimes, I found myself in positions where I had to be responsible. I remember very well the time, when I was still the tender age of five, my father's sister came to visit. I really loved my "Auntie," and she loved me too. I always wanted to be around her. One day, a day that has stayed in my mind for years, she took me downtown with her. I don't recall all the details of that day, but I remember the devastating parts. My Auntie got drunk and somehow stumbled into an old, closed-up train depot with hardwood boards that squeaked when you walked on them. I don't know why she went there, but I believe it was because she felt she couldn't walk straight and needed to rest. In any case, she lay down on the floor, and I sat beside her. After some time, I had to go to the bathroom and tried waking her. Unfortunately, I wet myself. I was really upset that I could not wake her, but I remembered the way we came in and left to get help. I remembered where the police station was and walked there. I told them that Auntie was in a squeaky house (referring to the boards on the floor) and that I could not wake her. Needless to say, I showed the police where she was and directed them to where I lived. Not realizing at the time that I had a responsibility to help her. I remember this story so well because throughout my years of growing up, my siblings and I often joked about the "squeaky house," now renovated as the Cumberland County Tourism Office.

As I grew older, around ten years of age, responsibilities increased. We had to "slop" (feed) the hogs with scraps from the table, gather eggs from the chicken coop (which I hated for fear of the chickens chasing me), water the garden, and gather and clean the vegetables. We were also responsible for cleaning the house, washing clothes, hanging them on the line outside to dry, bringing them in to be ironed, folded or hung, and put away. During the winter and spring months, hanging clothes on the line was challenging. In the winter, when it was freezing cold, the clothes would freeze and become stiff as soon as we started to pin them on the line. Our hands would get so cold that they would become numb. In the spring, no sooner would we get all the clothes on the line and go inside to rest from a hard day's work, it would start to rain. This meant running back outside to take the clothes off the line, especially if they had been hanging for a while and were almost dry; we didn't want them to get wet.

My mother taught us how to use a wash tub and scrub board to wash our clothes. By the time we finished, our knuckles were sore. Eventually, she was able to get a washing machine called a wringer washer. It had two rollers that looked like rolling pins pressed together to squeeze out water from the clothes. One person turned the crank, and the other person fed the clothes through the rollers. If we didn't remove our hand immediately after starting to feed the clothes through, we risked getting our fingers caught between the rollers.

Another task my sister and I were responsible for was cleaning the dishes after eating. My sister was taught to cook a full course meal at a young age, and she was a very good cook. My job was to set the table. My sister also washed dishes, and I dried and put them away. We had to be very careful not to break dishes. We understood that our parents couldn't afford to buy more. We were reminded many times why we should not waste food or break things because, as my father would say, "money don't grow on trees."

These early experiences laid the foundation for a career that would span from the fields of farm labor to the esteemed halls of the United States Department of Labor. Responsibility taught me reliability, foresight, and the importance of every role we play. It was a lesson that I carried with me, a guiding principle that has illuminated my path and prepared me for myriad challenges.

My parents lacked formal education and had no marketable job skills for well-paying jobs. My mother worked as a maid, providing cleaning and cooking services for a prominent lawyer and his family. My father worked as a truck driver for a small trucking company for minimum wage. Occasionally, he did odd jobs for a junkyard company and a glass company.

In the spring, summer, and early fall, my parents supplemented their low income by working for various area farmers. They picked strawberries, beans, tomatoes, peppers, cucumbers, removed the tops and bottoms from onions, and raked weeds from lettuce. At the time, I did not realize it, but my parents did their best to make an honest living and raise our family. On weekends, and when school closed for the summer, we had to help our parents work in the fields because they could not earn adequate wages with their regular jobs to support our family. It was what every poor family did.

My parents couldn't even afford to give us an allowance for treats. We learned to work for what we wanted. We collected empty soda bottles to exchange for money to buy two-for-a penny cookies and candy, and we worked in the fields to help buy our school clothes.

In the heartland of South Jersey, where the bean vines were wet from the early morning dew and the grounds sometimes muddy from overnight rain, my story takes root. The farm was more than just land; it was a classroom where life's most valuable lessons were taught.

As I reflect on my work-life, it was much like the process of a butterfly. In 1961, at the tender age of ten while I was in fifth grade, I began my work-life journey in the fields of farm labor, where I learned strong work ethics.

In the 1960s, farm labor paid low wages. I recall hearing my parents say farmers paid workers who picked their beans and other crops seventy-five cents a bushel basket, fifty cents for smaller baskets, and other farm labor hourly wage was, a dollar. It was through farm work that I learned the meaning of multi-tasking and meeting deadlines. There were many components to farm work. My father set a quota for each of us to pick so many baskets by the time he returned from his trucking job to join us for the remainder of the day. If we didn't meet the quota and deadline, the consequence was a beating you would never forget. It reminded me of what history says slaves went through when their masters beat them for not being productive working in the fields.

I hated farm labor. It was a hard and dirty job that required working long hours from sunup to sundown for low wages. We wore ugly work clothes — blue jeans or overalls, plaid shirts, and straw hats. These were considered farm clothes. To this day, I don't wear jeans; they still remind me of farm labor.

My mother could not afford to buy jeans from regular stores, so she bought them from Goodwill and Salvation Army. Jeans and overalls were used for farm work because they were practical and made of strong denim fabric. They were durable for farm work, which required crawling on our knees between two rows of wide green leafy vines, on hard and sometimes muddy ground with stones if it rained the night before. The pants were long and protected our legs from mosquito bites and other insects. I was always so embarrassed about looking like a farm laborer.

I remember one embarrassing day, while dressed in my farm attire and working on a field that was near home, the farmer said it was time to "knock off." That meant we were finished for the day. While walking home, a few guys in a convertible car passed me by. One of them yelled out, "Baby, don't let that farm work get you down." Then they laughed at me. It was obvious to them that I had been working on the farm because of the way I was dressed. Nowadays, jeans are considered fashionable, especially the holey ones with the knees and thighs ripped out. They remind me of the times Mom sewed patches over the holes to avoid buying another pair.

Sometimes while working, we were interrupted by a thunder and lightning storm. We had to seek shelter immediately to wait it out in our car, barn, or a farm house nearby. While waiting, it gave us a chance to rest. Sometimes listening to the rain pounding on the tin roof of a barn was scary, and other times, it was calming and put us to sleep, or we were just tired, especially after working most of the day. During the storm, Mom would make us "keep still and be quiet."

"God's working," she would say.

Our quietness demonstrated respect for God. Many times, when I was so tired, I thought to myself that God chose to work at the right time. Whenever I hear the rain and thunder, I'm reminded of those farm labor days when we had a chance to rest, hoping that it would rain all day.

I thought it was cruel to make children work in the fields, but it was understood, back then, that poor families needed their children to help earn a living. Years later, I learned that according to the United States Department of Labor (DOL), Fair Labor Standards Act, "Children under 12 are generally not permitted to work on farms not owned by their parents. However, children under 12 may work with parental consent outside of school hours." In addition, New Jersey state child labor laws say, "For children under 12, they can work on farms that are exempt from federal minimum wage provisions with written parental consent, and only if a parent is employed on the same farm." During those times, who knows whether farmers consulted with legal authorities to ensure they were in compliance with farm labor laws or restrictions and getting the permissions and appropriate paperwork before employing minors in farm labor. I'm sure my parents, like many other poor parents, were not concerned.

Some devastating memories from farm labor include when we were cutting the tops and bottoms off onions, and I accidentally slit the top of my thumb. It was so easy to do because of the way the onion had to be held to do the cutting. I carry that scar to this day. Another time, I was sitting on the farmer's tractor and touched a lever that brought down one of the blades on the top of my foot, causing a large cut on the opposite side of my ankle that required several stitches. Also, digging weeds away from lettuce with a hoe caused my hands to blister; we couldn't wear gloves, as it was difficult to grab hold to the hoe handle.

At the end of summer field work, my parents bought us brand new school clothes and shoes. However, if we still had our Buster Brown and Brogan shoes, there was no need for new shoes. Unless my parents had the extra money. Sometimes they went to Philly to shop for our school clothes, and other times they shopped at Mr. Big's and Two Guys department stores, Woolworths, or ordered from Sears and JC Penney Catalogs. I have fond memories of shopping for brand new clothes and shoes. I loved the scent of new shoes and the excitement of finding new outfits. When trying them on I would dance while looking at myself in the mirror.

In September when we went back to school, one of the things we had to do was stand before the class and give a presentation on what we did over the summer. I was always embarrassed to say I worked in the fields, so I just focused on the fun parts when we went to River View Beach Theme Park and visited my cousins in Philadelphia. That is where I could see the difference in the way poor country houses looked compared to city "row" houses. They had a doorbell, upstairs, basement, dining room, inside bathroom, and a small fenced-in backyard with no woods. I loved visiting them. They were relatives on my father's side. My uncle, who was my father's youngest brother, came from a different generation. He obviously had opportunities that gave him a better lifestyle than my father.

Experiencing city life had some dislikes. It was very noisy. Cars were constantly moving up and down the street, horns blowing, people talking loudly and hanging in the streets. While I enjoyed my city visits with my family, I liked the country for its peace and quiet, scenic views, and beautiful single-family homes with lovely front yard landscapes that I wished I had.

Chapter 2

BREAKING FREE:
THE JOURNEY FROM
DYSFUNCTION TO DISCOVERY

From humble beginnings, I learned the true meaning of struggle, hardship, fear, and survival. Raised in a dysfunctional home, my mother and father were unequally yoked, their personalities like night and day. Mom had a gentle, quiet spirit. She was kind and easy to talk to, slow to anger, liked nice things, clothes and hats, and always talked about wanting a nice home. On the other hand, my father was a man whose heart often appeared cold, controlling our lives with fear. He showed anger, never displayed or expressed love, but he kept a roof over our heads.

I used to believe my father had a mental problem because he was so quick-tempered. He overreacted to the smallest issue and punished severely. We were all fearful of him, including my mother. Just the sound of his heavy voice alone was scary — like the sudden sound of loud thunder and lightning cracking. It was worse when he was angry.

My father was not an alcoholic, nor did he take drugs. If he had, I could understand why he was so mean-spirited, but that was not the case. He was physically, verbally, and emotionally abusive. He was violent and spoke with such a loud, angry voice, as if he hated us. He was never loving or kind to my mother. I never heard him call her darling or any other loving name, and I never saw him hug or kiss her — not even on the cheek — or display any signs of affection and appreciation. He never complimented her or us. I only saw anger and out-of-control arguments. He was so mean that he wouldn't even allow us to go next door and play with our cousins.

I remember a particularly painful incident when my father tried to physically hurt me. I was about twelve years old. He gave me a chore to do, but I didn't fully understand and was scared he would get upset with me if I asked him to explain it again, because that has happened before. Apparently, I was taking too long to complete the task. He lost his patience with me *and* his temper. He yelled at me, called me an ugly name, and raised his hand to hit me. My reaction was to shield my face with my hands to block the hit. When he swung at me, I turned to run away, and he raised his foot to kick me, but I got away. The idea of him wanting to kick me hurt me.

My father had cut a long piece of tread out of a tire that he called a rubber hose and used it to beat us. He kept it conveniently near him, hanging on a hook on the wall above a chair where he sat. When we did something wrong, or something he disliked, there was no rational discussion. Instead, he quickly snatched down the rubber hose with force and anger and beat us with it. The way he beat us felt heartless, which is another painful memory I have. He grabbed us, put our head between his knees with our arms locked behind his legs so that we could not move, and beat us with the rubber hose. We were not bad or disrespectful kids to deserve that kind of punishment — no kids are. We were too scared of his reactions to do something so wrong to warrant those kinds of beatings. Yet he did it anyway. Again, as if he hated us.

Before my father created his whipping rubber hose, he would beat us with a switch that he cut off a tree in the backyard. However, the switch was more like a branch. He found the largest and thickest limb, stripped off the leaves, and snapped off some of the smaller attached branches, which stood out like little thorns lined up on the branch. Just the idea of knowing we were going to get a beating made our hearts pound extremely fast as a result of fear. When he walked towards us to take a swing, seeing him coming with anger in his eyes, the instinct was to run. I was the running child. I refused to stand still and allow myself to be beaten unmercifully. So I tried to get away from him. I suppose he was just as much out of breath running after me as I was running away. Needless to say, he caught me, and when he finished beating me, I had large welts on my back, arms, and legs. My brother used to tell me to stop running and get it over with because it made my father angrier, especially when the first thing he would say in a hateful, loud, screaming voice was, "Don't you run from me, gal." I did it anyway.

My father beat us so long and with full force behind every swing that sometimes the switch would break. That's the reason he came up with another method — the rubber hose. I hated him for the way he beat us. I went to school with visible welts on my legs and tried to hide them with long socks. But I could not hide what I was feeling in my head or my heart. I hurt so deeply emotionally that it was difficult to concentrate in school. I suffered in silence, never showing it.

My father mistreated my older brother and sister worse than he did the rest of us. I recall one time when my father got so angry with my older brother that he hit him with a broom handle. At age sixteen, he ran away from home. He was sick and tired of being physically and emotionally abused. He had a difficult time trying to make it on his own, especially since he was a slow learner and had to drop out of school, but he broke free of that dysfunctional home and ultimately discovered a better way of life and became a self-made businessman repairing electrical appliances.

It was not easy living in a dysfunctional home. If this type of beating was happening in these days and times, it would be considered child abuse. We were not aware of any laws preventing child abuse when we were growing up. I suppose some people would say, why did my mother allow this to happen? Well, she was afraid of him hurting her too, and sometimes she was not at home; she was working. However, there were times when Mom tried to stop my father or say something to prevent him from beating us, he would get angry and threaten her. Timid as she was, she would back down in fear. It was understandable to me. If she tried to make him stop and he hurt her, we would be left alone with him. I believe her presence prevented him from doing worse because there were times, as scared as we were, we could see she was trembling nervously while saying, "That's enough!"

I don't recall my mother ever whipping us, except once when my youngest brother was playing outside with his friends and did not want to come inside. After calling him several times, he reluctantly came inside and angrily shouted at Mom. When she turned to speak to him, he hurriedly walked away and went into the bathroom, slamming the door in her face. Immediately, she opened the door and spanked him several times. He got the message that he was being disrespectful to her and never did that again — a lesson learned that we all witnessed.

I never saw my mother be abusive to any of my siblings or me. Mom was not a violent person. She was humble, kind, loving, and spiritual. She didn't like arguments; instead, she was more of a *looker*. When she gave us a certain look and tightened her lips, we knew we had either said or done something wrong and straightened up. She might give a few warning words, but that was the extent of her display of disappointment in us.

We tried to find some enjoyment in our home. The only time my father was relaxed that I can remember was during birthdays. He allowed us to have birthday parties. When we worked in the fields, we had extra money to have birthday parties for my sister, my father, my two brothers, and my mother.

In May, we celebrated my sister's birthday. It marked the beginning of the parties. We always had a full house of kids from school, the neighborhood, and family dancing and having fun. Mom bought a big sheet cake from the bakery, and we had ice cream, potato chips, peanuts, pretzels, and other typical party delights. We showed off all the latest dances we saw on Dick Clark's "American Bandstand" and really enjoyed these happy times.

In July, we celebrated my father's birthday, and in September, my two older brothers' birthdays. It was a double celebration. People came from all across town. Cars were lined up from the beginning to the end of our street. Then in November, we had a birthday party for my mother. Her birthday was the last party of the year. For every birthday party, we had the same crowd, but at some point, word got around, and the crowd got larger each year.

My youngest brother and I never had a birthday party. His birthday was in December, just two days before Christmas, and my birthday, in January, came after Christmas when winter struck hard. There was no extra money, and besides, it was always either a snowstorm or knee-deep snow on the ground that prevented people from coming out. However, my brother and I never complained because we just looked forward to those happy times and enjoyed the planning process for our family's birthdays. We helped with the decorations, menu, and selected the latest records, practiced new dance steps, and prepared for the fun.

In 1963, when I was about twelve years old, an unfortunate situation happened. Looking from the kitchen window, I saw my brother do something outside, and I told him that it was wrong and that it reminded me of what I saw our father do—urinating behind a tree like a dog. He could have used the outside toilet that we still had. My brother and I had an ugly argument about it, and when my father came home, my brother told him what I said, which caused a serious problem.

My mother, sister, and I were in the kitchen snapping beans that we had brought home from the bean field. My father entered the kitchen, and without any words or warning, he walked up to me and slapped me so hard that I fell to the floor. I screamed and my mother yelled, "Don't hit her no more!"

Simultaneously, everything happened: my father swung around to my mother, picked up a chair, raised it, and as he began to bring it down on her, he yelled, "You don't tell me what to do."

I screamed.

My brother grabbed the chair and said, "I'm not going to let you hit Mom with this chair!"

My sister screamed and threw a pan of beans that hit him on the head. They saved mom's life. My father yelled at my sister and charged at her. She immediately ran out the door with no shoes on her feet, wearing jeans and a green shell top. My father ran after her, but never caught her and we never saw her again for almost three years. It was a good thing we did not have any guns because someone would have been shot or killed.

The way my sister had to leave home was so unfortunate. I hated that I caused a devastating situation. However, as years passed, I realized that it was probably the only way she could leave that dysfunctional hellhole of a house and discover a new life for herself. It turned out that the situation that had caused her to leave home was a blessing in disguise.

Nothing was the same anymore. Although my sister and I were not close in age to share talks and do things together, I missed her. The parties continued, but there was still a void that we needed to fill. My brother and I loved singing, and during our generation we grew up with Motown music. Like most cities, kids imitated the Motown singing groups. When we were in junior high school, my brother sang with about three guys, and they sang and danced like the Temptations. My cousin, Carolyn, and my friend, Louise, and I formed a three-part harmony a cappella group and called ourselves "The Crownetts." We wore tiaras on our heads to reflect our name when we performed at school parties and talent shows. My cousin was the lead singer, and she could really sing. Louise and I did background with perfect harmony. Louise had a strong and smooth alto voice, and I was a high-pitched soprano. Everyone loved our group and looked forward to seeing us perform. We lived on the same street and walked to school. While walking, we practiced our choreography and sang our favorite songs by the Supremes, Marvelettes, and a few other female groups. By the time we arrived at school, we were ready to perform if we had to. This brought peace to my mind, pleasure to my ears, and filled a void.

We learned to sing in Buckshutem Elementary School. Our fifth-grade teacher, Ms. Madison, taught us how to sing using our diaphragm. She played piano for special events, and I recall her asking me to sing "God Bless America" in class. I was nervous standing in front of the class, but I got through it. Each day, after reading a Bible verse, we always saluted the flag and sang the Star-Spangled Banner. Music and singing were the best part of going to school for me. Studying was a chore that required concentration, which sometimes I couldn't manage because of the situation I was dealing with at home.

When I was about fourteen years old, I started developing as a young lady, and my father started touching me, which made me feel uncomfortable. I knew he was not being a loving father because that wasn't who he was. It seemed strange to me when he put his arm around my shoulder and across my chest as he walked past. Other times, when I was standing by the kitchen sink, he would brush against me as if the walkway was narrow when it was not.

Another time, I recall he actually touched my breast, and I jerked away and looked at him with hatred in my eyes as he walked away. I knew then for sure what he was doing, and from that point on, whenever I saw him coming, I moved out of his way.

While picking peppers in the fields, my father came over to me and whispered what he would do to me if he ever caught me by myself. That was the last straw. At first, I was afraid to tell anyone what he said. I suffered in silence. I was afraid to sleep at night, and my schoolwork suffered. I was mentally and emotionally drained from his harassment for months and was sick of it.

I had planned to run away, but I didn't want to leave my Mom. Finally, I decided to tell my aunt Doll and Mom what he had been doing and saying to me. Mom was afraid to approach him about it, and I begged her not to for fear of what he might do to her. However, she told me to hold on and be careful not to be around him alone. In the meantime, I walked to and from school with my friend Louise, and stayed close to my brothers. I didn't know at the time, but I believed that Mom and my aunt, at some point, communicated and came up with a plan to get away. I recently learned that a neighbor and friend of Mom's from the "back street" where we lived contributed to the plan. It has been a mystery that was never discussed or uncovered.

In November 1966, I came home from school one day and found a stranger, but a nice lady, visiting our home. My mother referred to her as "Mother Oreola," a spiritual woman. I had never heard Mom speak of her before, but suddenly she was there. Mom told me that she was there to help us escape. Not knowing at that time how they were going to pull it off, I followed instructions. Mom said my father would pick me up from school and bring me home and to not be afraid. I still did not know what she and "Mother Oreola" had planned, but I trusted them. Obviously, they didn't want me to know for fear that he might try to get information from me.

The next day, after I went to school as usual, when the time came for me to leave early, I went to Louise's class room. Standing in the hallway outside of her classroom door, I got her attention. Whispering to avoid her teacher seeing and hearing me, I tried telling her that I had to leave town, but I don't think she could hear what I was saying. I didn't want to leave my friend without saying goodbye. Just when our singing group was progressing, I had to give it up. We were in tenth grade and had been in school together since kindergarten. She had become my sister and I was hoping we would graduate together too.

My father picked me up from school and told me that mom had been sick and that "Mother Oreola" came to take her away to get well and that Mom needed me to be with her. It was then that I realized this was the plan to get away and never return. My father drove us to the airport, not knowing he would never see us again. We secretly left New Jersey and flew to Ohio.

After years of enduring a dysfunctional home and working hard in the fields, Mom finally broke free, taking me with her but leaving my two brothers behind. She had tried to leave before, but always returned. My father had known she would. I recall one morning, after my father left for work, I found a large knife under the pillow where he had slept on the sofa the night Mom left. It was clear he intended to harm her if she returned that night. I never told anyone, fearing the consequences. The impact of living in such an environment made me vow never to marry or have children, afraid I would face the same mistreatment and my children would suffer as well.

Ohio began an odyssey of travels for Mom and me, going from city to city, living with and depending on different people (sometimes strangers) to help us start a new life. Now, it was just Mom and me with an indescribable bond. We stayed with the spiritual lady that night, and the next day, she explained that she had made arrangements for us to stay with a friend until we could decide what we wanted to do and where we wanted to go. She put us on a bus to Cincinnati.

"Mother Thomlinson," another spiritual lady, met us at the bus terminal and took us to her home. It was a beautiful, large four-level mansion that was used as a boarding house with apartments inside. Some people rented apartments, and some rented rooms. It was an amazing house. The rooms were all very large, beautifully decorated, and the house had several entrances. My mother and I shared a large room together.

We talked many nights about what we needed to do and how uncomfortable we were living with strangers. They were all very nice and kind, but we felt confined to the house and church, which we attended almost every night. Not that going to church often was a problem, it's just that we were nervous about deciding where to go. We knew that going back home was *not* an option, and neither did we want to go back. We felt my father had figured out, by now, that after he could not reach us by phone to see if we had arrived safely, that the woman who helped us get away had given him a fake contact number. We heard that he contacted the authorities and told them that we were kidnapped, and they were looking for us.

Living in the house with "Mother Thomlinson" was actually a nice change. We didn't have to do anything. We had maid service and a very good cook. All of that was fine, but we had no real purpose living there, especially since we understood from the beginning that it was temporary and just a place to plan our future, which had to be done quickly.

By late November 1966, we had been with "Mother Thomlinson" for a few weeks and we were restless. Mom tried to get financial support for me from social services, but they required information that would have meant contacting my father. Aunt Doll contacted Aunt Hazel who lived in Washington, D.C., and they made arrangements for us to stay with her and her family. So, we were back on a Greyhound Bus and moving to Washington, D.C. By December, I had not been in school for about a month. Mom enrolled me in Spingarn High School, but I attended night school. I don't recall why I couldn't enroll in regular daytime classes, but I believe it was because Mom feared requesting my records from Bridgeton High School would reveal our location.

Mom was unable to work due to problems with her hip, resulting from a fall she experienced when she was a young girl. Her parents had never taken her to the doctor, so she had suffered in pain for years. My aunt helped Mom apply for social services and made us feel welcome. We stayed with my aunt and her family for a couple of months, but Mom decided that with the small check we were receiving from social services, we could not afford to live in D.C. Besides, my aunt did all she could to help us. She never complained, but we realized she had a husband and a young family — it was time to give them a break from house guests.

Before the spring of 1967, Mom contacted my aunt Mable in Montclair, New Jersey, and made arrangements for us to live with her until we could get a place of our own. We stayed with my aunt for a few days, and she helped Mom get a one-bedroom apartment. I was able to enroll in tenth grade at Montclair High School and met several friends. Things were beginning to shape up for us. I was so grateful for the help that all my aunts extended to Mom and me. Her sisters demonstrated the true meaning of family being there for you in time of need.

I decided to get a part-time job to help Mom out with rent and food. I worked after school at a TV repair and music record shop. It was my first real job other than farm work. I had a huge responsibility and was confident I would do well since I learned the meaning of responsibility early on. The record shop provided on-the-job training, and I learned how to communicate well with people, including irate customers, operate a cash register, recorded the number of sales made for the day, and respond to telephone inquiries. I enjoyed working at the music record shop. Playing all of the Motown records for customers brought back fond memories of the birthday parties we had at our house.

I had a clear frame of mind, studied well, and passed to the 11th grade. When school closed for the summer, I continued working at the record shop. I enjoyed my summer job, being around music, and dressing nicely for work. This was a welcome change from doing farm work. Earning extra money that summer helped Mom and me get a better apartment. Mom found a two-bedroom apartment in Newark, New Jersey, and we moved near my aunt Doll. We did fine for a couple of months. We even located my sister, and she and her baby boy came to live with us. I continued working at the record shop, but I had to commute by bus into Montclair, New Jersey. With traffic, the commute was about a forty-five minute to an hour ride from where we lived, and it took too long to get to work and back home. I decided to quit the job I really enjoyed for a job closer to where I lived.

I quickly got a job working for a single mother in a lovely private home in the suburbs of Newark. I was responsible for babysitting an infant about three months old and doing light housework, dusting, and cleaning floors. It was important for me to communicate clearly with the mother to understand her instructions and expectations and any additional tasks I was responsible for. To avoid mistakes and ensure I heard her correctly, I repeated her instructions for approval. A lesson I learned from that incident with my father when he tried to kick me because I misunderstood what I was supposed to do. Being adaptable and attentive to the child's needs was key to being a successful babysitter.

In early August 1967, Mom and I learned that my father was spotted in the area. We believe he was informed by the authorities who probably traced our location through mail from social services payments Mom was receiving. We didn't know where else we could go, but we knew we could not go back home and had to leave before he found us.

Mom and one of her sisters communicated with their cousin in Salisbury, Maryland, and they made arrangements for us to live with her and her husband. They had a two-bedroom bungalow and welcomed us to come. I was so tired of packing and moving. I felt like a fugitive. Actually, that's exactly what we were — except we were not criminals and had done nothing wrong. Just when we thought we were settled, we were off running again. We left everything we had in the apartment, took only our clothes, got on the Greyhound Bus again, and moved to Salisbury, Maryland. My sister went back to Washington, D.C.

Salisbury, Maryland, was a small country town, much like my hometown—Bridgeton. We lived in the same type of neighborhood— all African American, low income, and low educated. However, people were friendly, and the neighborhood was clean and decent with poor people doing the best they could. Mom and I shared a room, and her cousin introduced her to some friends in the neighborhood. Mom Joined St. James AME Church where most adults attended, and I joined First Baptist Church and the church choir. I enjoyed singing during services.

In September, mom enrolled me in eleventh grade at Wicomico Senior High School. Making friends at this school was challenging. Coming from the North, I was used to going to interracial schools, so I always had Caucasian and African American classmates and friends. In Salisbury, some African American students I made friends with didn't want me to be friends with the Caucasians and vice versa. I was always faced with difficult decisions, but the way I dealt with this issue was simply to be friends with whomever accepted me as a friend. I used my judgment and let my conscience be my guide instead of allowing others to guide me. It worked for me, and I adjusted.

I met girls in my neighborhood and walked to the school bus stop with them. I wore nice clothes to school, and some of the girls commented that I dressed like a teacher, spoke "proper," and called me "Ms. 500." Sometimes I ignored their comments because they didn't know where I came from or how Mom and I were making it. Other times, I rolled my eyes at them and turned my head. Mom had started getting social services for both of us and was able to buy nice dresses for me. They were not from the finer stores, but they were not from

Goodwill either. I told Mom that the kids were picking on me because I wore nice dresses to school. She said, "Just because we are poor, that doesn't mean we have to look like it, so you be the example." Words of wisdom I treasure to this day.

I got involved in school activities, joined the girls' drill team, practiced our drill after school, sang in the school choir and talent shows, performed at football games, and had a lot of fun. I discovered the meaning of *peace of mind*.

One of my classmates in my music class heard me sing, and he invited me to sing with his thirteen-piece band called the "Soul Expressions." It was an interracial group, and I enjoyed singing with them. We performed at school programs and other events. After a few months, one of the guys approached and propositioned me. I felt if I could not become a successful singer based on my talent and ability, I would not have it any other way. I was not going to sleep around or take drugs to fit in, so I left the band and I changed my career interest.

Meanwhile, Mom and I had to move from her cousin's house. Her husband was an alcoholic, and one day he made a pass at me. I told Mom, and she told her cousin. She confronted her husband about it, and he said we had to move. We moved in with another one of Mom's cousins. I know she was just as tired of moving as I was, but she never once complained.

During the summer of 1968, I was trying to find a job to help out, but it was difficult. Under unfortunate circumstances, I met a social worker Ms. Jones and shared what my Mom and I were going through. She knew a school teacher who was the Program Director for the We Care Summer Program

and told him about our situation. He hired me to work as his assistant—answering phones, taking messages, receiving applications for enrollment, and typing brief letters to parents explaining the program. The We Care Program was a community initiative providing support and activities for youth during the summer. The program included a variety of recreational, educational, and enrichment activities designed to engage youth in a safe and nurturing environment during the school break. This was my first office job. I had a desk in the Director's office, and even though it was summer, and the enrollees wore their We Care Program uniform T-Shirts, I still dressed professionally for the office. My supervisor often complemented me on my professional look and work ethics at such a young age, a lesson I learned from my teachers, to dress well and "look the part." My strong work ethics were learned from farm labor.

When the We Care program was over for the summer, the Director asked me to sign his name on the program certificates. He said I had beautiful penmanship and took a picture of me. That was a memorable moment — I felt valued the way all the team leaders in the program made every youth feel, some like me from broken homes.

After a few weeks of staying with Mom's cousin Josephine, we left and stayed with Ms. Jones who contacted the Wicomico County Housing Authority to inquire about housing for Mom and me. We had an opportunity to live in a newly developed "Section 8" housing project. I helped Mom apply for an apartment but learned it required three years of Salisbury residency. This was very disappointing, as we had only been living in the area for about a year.

When the summer program ended, an opportunity for another singing job opened for me. One day, a man who had heard me sing at an event with the Soul Expressions' band remembered me. He was the manager of a band called the "Mighty Exciters" and asked if I would be interested in singing with his band. He invited me to their show to meet the band members. I was impressed and accepted the offer. I sang rhythm and blues on weekends in nightclubs and at special events. I enjoyed it so much that at one time, I wanted to be a professional singer.

Mom knew that I loved music and that singing was my dream. She was a prayer warrior and always prayed that God would lead and guide me to do the right things and live a decent life. She was never concerned about my singing in nightclubs, as she trusted me to carry myself like a lady no matter where I was. With all the sacrifices she made for me, I would not dare disappoint her. She met all the guys in the band, and they assured her that they would take care of me. The band was booked with "gigs" every weekend, and I enjoyed it.

One day, I was thinking about my older sister and brother, wondering where they were and how they were doing. I suddenly remembered that Mom used to live in Salisbury years ago and that my older sister and brother were born there, with three years age difference between them. I reminded Mom, she explained that to Ms. Jones, and they went back to the Housing Authority where Mom presented my sibling's birth certificates as proof that she had lived in Salisbury for more than three years. Her application for housing was accepted and immediately we moved into our new one-bedroom apartment. To God be the glory!

My singing job enabled me to earn enough money to furnish our apartment. At seventeen years old, I opened a furniture account with Feldman Brothers furniture company and purchased a really nice 5-piece kitchen table set, sofa and chair set, twin beds, TV, stereo, and other household furnishings. I enjoyed helping Mom decorate our new home. Decorating was a skill that came natural for me. We were happy and settled in our own home. We located my sister and she and her two little children came to live with us. We were happy to have them with us and later, she was blessed with a nice place of her own as well.

In September 1968, my senior year, I joined the majorettes' team. We performed in parades and at football games. I was so involved in my extracurricular school activities that my homework and studying for exams suffered to the extent that I was asked to leave the majorettes' team. The rule was we had to maintain a "C" average to participate in extracurricular activities. I was heartbroken. My studies suffered because I was working. However, I understood that I had to get my grades up, especially in English, in order to graduate. I realized that nothing was more important to me than graduating. After all Mom and I had been through, I wanted to make her proud.

THE PATH OF PROFESSIONAL GROWTH: CLIMBING THE LADDER OF SUCCESS

On June 6, 1969, I graduated high school. I am grateful to the late Reverend Mills Pastor of First Baptist Church in Salisbury, Maryland. He was my Pastor and he did not hesitate to purchase my class picture when I asked for assistance. Mom couldn't afford to purchase all the keep sakes that graduates want. Money was limited to the bare necessities — food, shelter and clothes. However, she purchased my class ring. Years later, I purchased my class yearbook.

This part of my memoir is more than a chronicle of jobs held; it is an account of personal growth and the relentless pursuit of self-improvement.

As a high school student, I stood at the crossroads of adulthood, aware that the path to higher education was obstructed by financial barriers. Yet, I knew the importance of academic diligence; good grades were not just letters on a report card, but keys to unlocking doors when college tuition was a luxury beyond reach. Mom, a beacon of strength, could not offer the financial support for college, and at the time we were not aware of special programs to assist disadvantaged families with college tuition, but Mom had provided me with the tools of determination and faith.

The early days were marked by a quest for purpose, a search for a job that was not merely a means to an end, but a stepping-stone to greater opportunities. From retail to hospitality, clerical work to community service, each role was an apprenticeship in the art of survival and a lesson in the economics of self-sufficiency. It was through these on-the-job training experiences that I learned the most valuable lesson of all: the dignity of labor and the pricelessness of education. Years of dedication allowed me to fund my own college tuition, an achievement that was both a challenge and a triumph. This journey was not just about earning degrees; it was about evolving into a person capable of contributing to society, and eventually, to the United States Department of Labor. My work life journey was like the progress of a butterfly — I started as one thing and became something else.

In the tapestry of my life, each thread represents a step, a job, a lesson learned. From the humble beginnings of *farm labor*, where the soil taught me the value of hard work and patience, to *motel maid*, to the busy corridors of *retail*, where every sale was a story and every customer, a new chapter. My journey weaves through the melodies of *singing*, the precision of *decorating*, and the creativity of *event planning*. Each role, from *clerical* to *motel maid*, from *assistant credit manager* to *floral designer*, has been a brushstroke in the masterpiece of my career. As I transitioned into roles such as *staff assistant, workforce development specialist,* and *grants and contracts project manager,* I gathered not just skills but also wisdom. It was these experiences that paved the way to my role as *Employment Law Advisor* at the U.S. Department of Labor. This memoir, is not just a recounting of jobs held; it is a celebration of growth, resilience, and the unwavering hope that propels us forward.

After graduating from high school, I needed to find a job to support Mom and me. The social service support payments Mom received for me stopped when I turned 18, leaving us to rely solely on her small monthly disability checks. I wasn't sure what I wanted to do, but I remembered my Aunt Hazel's words. She had also worked hard in the fields as a child, and when it was time for her job search, she said, "I didn't know what I wanted to do, but I knew what I was not going to do." She was referring to not doing farm labor anymore. I could relate to her sentiment and felt the same way. This taught me the process of elimination when trying to make decisions. With only a high school education, I knew my job opportunities were limited.

My first job after high school was in the hospitality industry as a maid at the Statesman Motel in Salisbury, Maryland. It certainly wasn't the job for me—cleaning toilets, vacuuming floors, making beds, emptying dirty, smelly ashtrays, and going from one room to another doing the exact same thing. After a few hours of working, I wanted to quit, but it was an honest job, and I needed the money to help Mom. So, I held on long enough to get a two-week paycheck and then applied for a job with Manpower Employment Agency. They find jobs for prospective employees and send them out to various positions, some temporary and some full-time. With only a high school education, I was limited in getting the better jobs. I was sent to Perdue Chicken Factory to work as an office assistant doing basic office work. That job was a two-week temporary assignment until their regular employee returned to work.

Another job I was assigned to was at an insurance company, where I served as the office receptionist. I was responsible for greeting customers, answering phones, and taking messages. This assignment was also temporary.

I found a full-time job on my own in the retail industry at Benjamins Department store. I learned about fine china, crystal, how to arrange designer towels, and professional gift wrapping. I continued singing on the weekends until I lost interest. The glamor and excitement was fading. It became too demanding and required dedication to learning new songs and practicing every minute of the day to be ready for rehearsals and performances. I also let the job at Benjamins go. It was just a job where I learned new skills. With every job I took, I improved my skills and built a foundation of experience that would one day support my ambitions. I still didn't know what I wanted to do, I just knew that I would know it when it felt right to me. Until then, I had to keep climbing. So, I left Salisbury in search of a dream job.

That summer, I moved to Philadelphia and lived with my Aunt Betty Walker and family. Aunt Betty helped me find a job at Sears

& Roebuck catalog department doing clerical work as a clerk-typist processing catalog orders in a typing pool. The orders were submitted on what looked like post cards with names and addresses. Each order had to be typed into a computerized system and we were expected to process so many a day with deadlines. I was able to meet my quota as I learned earlier from working in the fields. I didn't stay there long as I lost interest and went back to Salisbury until I decided to leave again.

In January 1970, I was 19 years old and like most teens not sure what I wanted to do. I decided to move to Newark, New Jersey where I lived with my cousin for a few months. Desperate to find a job, my retail experience lead me to a telemarketing company selling light bulbs. It was amazing to me to see the operations of a telemarketer. I vividly recall that it was a large open room with employees sitting at a desk with a telephone and what looked like a gigantic folder standing on the desk in front of the worker. The folder was actually a script to follow when talking on the phone to prospective customers.

One of the instructions stated that if the customer hangs up on you, call them back immediately and say, "I'm sorry we got disconnected. We had a bad connection." I was good at speaking to people, however, I got tired of being hung up on. One day when I followed the instructions when customers hang up, the person said, "No, there was no bad connection, I hung up on you and don't call back." They hung up again. It was then that I felt I had enough and this type of job was not for me. However, I stayed long enough to get a two-week paycheck while looking for something else.

This experience of my career journey led me to the public administration industry. I was employed by the New Jersey State Employment Office within the labor market information and workforce development area where I joined the Work Incentive (WIN) Program Division. The WIN program was a pivotal initiative aimed at motivating and assisting individuals in their job search endeavors. As a Receptionist, I was at the forefront of this mission, providing the first point of contact for clients entering our office. This role was my introduction to the professional office environment, demanding a blend of interpersonal skills and administrative expertise. My responsibilities included answering phones, managing application intake, and coordinating with case managers to ensure efficient client service. On days when case managers were unavailable, I stepped in to bridge the gap, engaging with clients to understand their needs, informing them about the WIN Program, and distributing educational materials.

The position required a dynamic personality, effective communication, and a professional demeanor — qualities that I perfected diligently. It was a role that challenged me to learn swiftly, comprehend complex information, and convey it succinctly to a diverse audience. These skills and experience proved invaluable as they laid the groundwork, and prepared me for, my later success as an Employment Law Advisor with the U.S. Department of Labor.

In this elevated capacity, I drew upon my experience from the state employment office, applying my ability to quickly grasp and interpret employment laws and regulations. My role evolved to advising employers on legal requirements and informing workers of their rights under the Worker Adjustment and Retraining Notification (WARN) Act, reflecting a significant progression from my early days of direct client interaction to shaping policy and guiding compliance at a national level.

In January 1971, I turned a new page in my life's journey, leaving behind the New Jersey State Employment Office to return to Salisbury, Maryland. This move was driven by personal aspirations, but upon realizing that certain relationships were not conducive to my growth, I chose to pursue a path of progress and self-improvement.

I embraced a secretarial role in the educational services with the Board of Education at Salisbury Elementary School, a position that marked a significant shift in my career. In the bustling environment of the principal's office, I was entrusted with typical secretarial duties: typing, filing, copying, and managing phone communications. My voice became a familiar echo over the PSA system, announcing events and safety protocols with precision and clarity.

This role was more than administrative—it was a reminder of my cherished elementary school days and the teachers who inspired me. Their professionalism and eloquence sparked a desire within me to pursue teaching. Although my career took a different direction, the importance of articulate speech they instilled in me became a cornerstone for my professional interactions, from job interviews to public speaking engagements.

The cyclical nature of the academic year brought summers of retail work at WT Grants, a department store where I improved my customer service skills and organizational ability. I also got a part-time evening job working at the mall for Learner Shops, a ladies retail store. I learned about style and color coordination. The role at Lerner Shops further diversified my experience, introducing me to the world of fashion — a passion that has stayed with me to this day.

These experiences, each unique and formative, were threads woven into the fabric of my career. They taught me adaptability, the value of clear communication, and the joy of lifelong learning. As I reflect on these roles, I see not just jobs but stepping-stones that led me to become an advocate for workers' rights and a voice of guidance in the realm of employment law.

In June 1972, I bid farewell to Salisbury Elementary School, determined to seek a career that offered more than the secretarial role I had known. Salisbury, with its small-town limits, could not offer the advancement I sought. Inspired by my Aunt Hazel's encouragement and her own federal career she once knew, I went to Philadelphia and stayed a few weeks with her for guidance. She was always willing to welcome me into her home and in sharing her wisdom.

With my federal SF-171 application meticulously typed by my aunt, she encouraged me to apply for a federal government career. I learned that they could assist with job related training. This knowledge, coupled with my diverse work history, fueled my determination to pursue a career in Washington, D.C. I returned to Salisbury to share my aspirations with Mom, whose prayers and blessings, along with a glowing alarm clock, and a Bible marked at Psalm 27, became my luck charms for the journey ahead.

August 1972 marked the beginning of my quest for a fulfilling career with advancement opportunities and benefits. In other words, a dream job, where I could be valued and make a positive difference. With just $50 and a heart full of ambition, I stepped into Washington, D.C., ready to climb the federal government's ladder. Despite the absence of a college degree, my experiences from farm labor to various industries instilled me with confidence.

My initial days in D.C. were challenging, navigating the uncertainties of a new city and seeking a safe haven. An unsettling encounter at a rooming house led me to seek refuge with a family friend, affirming my belief in my mother's protective prayers.

When I arrived in D.C., I went to the ladies, Young Women's Christian Association, and sat in the living area long enough to read the newspapers for a room and board house. As much as I did not want to stay with strangers, I had no choice, especially not knowing the D.C. areas and I didn't have enough money to stay at the "Y." I found a place with a small family — husband, wife, and two children. I explained my situation about looking for a job, and we chatted a little about ourselves to get to know each other. Then I was shown my room.

Later that night while sleeping, I was awaken by a noise at my door that scared me. I had the door locked. I yelled out, "Who's there?" The man of the house whispered his name and said he was just checking to see if I was ok. I said "yes, thank you" and looked at the clock that mom gave me; it was glowing in the dark at 3:00 a.m. I became suspicious and felt very uncomfortable. I couldn't get back to sleep and didn't try to. So I sat up and stayed up thinking if anyone would check on me, it should be the lady of the house, not her husband. It did not make sense to me, especially at that time of the night or early morning.

When the sun rose, I got dressed in my "Sunday Best" and went to look for a church. I discovered the Vermont Avenue Baptist Church was a few blocks away. There I stayed for most of the day. I feared going back to the house and feared telling the lady what her husband did, so later that afternoon, I called my sister in Salisbury and told her what happened. She suggested I call a friend of hers who lived across the Maryland line and ask if I could stay with her. I did and she picked me up at church, took me back to the rooming house to get my clothes, and took me back to stay at her apartment until I found a job. It was clear that Mom's prayers were with me.

For several days I embarked on a job hunt that took me through the many corridors of federal agencies, walking from one agency to another distributing my applications and envisioning a future filled with opportunities. It was amazing to see so many federal government buildings. I was like a child in a candy store, thinking *so many to choose from*. I fell in love with the idea of becoming a federal employee in Washington, D.C.

One day, I was tired from a long day of job searching and, while waiting at the bus stop to go back to the apartment, a Chinese man walked up and started to make conversation. I recall him saying, "You look tired." I was and could barely smile, but I did and told him I was tired because I had been job searching all day. He suggested that I take the Q2 or Q7 bus to the National Institutes of Health (NIH) in Bethesda, Maryland and that they were hiring. He explained NIH came under the United States Health Education and Welfare (HEW) agency now known as Health and Human Services.

The next day, I couldn't wait to take the bus to NIH. I left several applications and roamed the halls getting a feel for where things were. A few days later, I was called for a job interview.

My dream came true! After several interviews where I showcased my skills and experiences, I was offered a position with the U.S. Department of HEW, Public Health Service, at NIH in the Training and Education Branch. In general, it focused on providing training programs, educational resources, and professional development opportunities to improve public health practices and outcomes. Finally, I believed this is where I wanted to be.

On August 6, 1972, I started my federal career as a General Schedule (GS)-2 Clerk-Typist with an annual salary of $5,000 and yearly promotions up to a GS-5. Basically, GS is a primary pay scale for federal government employees.

The GS is divided into 15 grades. GS-1 to 4 is entry level and requires a high school diploma or equivalent. GS covers job types, including administrative, professional, technical, and clerical positions. I embraced the challenge with enthusiasm, marking the beginning of a roller coaster journey that would see me rise through the ranks to a WARN Act Policy/Employment Law Advisor GS-13 with a six-figure salary. My determination, faith, resilience, and my mother's prayers, ever-present, continued to guide me through each step of my climb to victory.

I was responsible for typing a variety of documents from handwritten drafts in which insertions, deletions, corrections, and references were made and which involved a variety of formats, including difficult tabulation for the final product. I assisted in the preparation of correspondence, studies, and reports, by abstracting readily accessible information from designated sources and compiling and assembling as required. Made copies of various documents. Filed and withdrew material arranged in alphabetical, numerical, subject-matter, or similar system. Assisted in the maintenance of office records by selecting pertinent information from designated sources and posting to appropriate logs. Received and distributed mail. Received incoming calls and visitors and referred to appropriate staff member or took messages in their absence.

After 2 weeks of working at NIH, I earned my first paycheck and found a cute studio apartment within walking distance of NIH. A few years later, I moved into a lovely two-bedroom, government subsidized apartment in Rockville, Maryland, until I could afford something better. This apartment was more affordable, allowing me to save money and send some home to Mom. Over the years, every residential move I made was bigger and better.

I have never borrowed money from anyone. To supplement my GS-2 income, I worked at Hot Shops Restaurant near my studio apartment, working three nights a week from 6:00 p.m. to 10:00 p.m. in the kitchen making sandwiches. My work hours at NIH were 8:30 a.m. to 5:00 p.m., and the part-time hours were perfect. I was independent and doing exceptionally well.

In 1973, my combination of full-time and part-time jobs enabled me to purchase my first car, a brand new Chevy Camaro. Now that I had a car, I could drive to Vermont Avenue Baptist Church in Washington, D.C., where I became a member. Raised with a deep belief in God, my faith has been the compass that guided me through life's journey. As a devoted member, I lent my voice to the choir and shared my knowledge as a Sunday school teacher. In later years, I served as the church decorator for holidays and special events. These roles not only enriched my spiritual life but also allowed me to touch the lives of others in meaningful ways.

Seeking a higher-paying part-time job, I resigned from Hot Shoppes Restaurant and began working evenings in retail at the Hecht Company department store in Montgomery Mall, in Bethesda, Maryland. It was exciting to see that everything was falling into place for me.

Initially I was hired as a sales associate, my duties included operating the cash register for cash and credit card transactions and assisting customers in various departments. When not at the register, I maintained the linen and towel department, ensuring it was neat and organized. My supervisor was consistently impressed with my performance and frequently praised my work.

After a few weeks, a position opened in the credit office, and my supervisor recommended me for the role of assistant credit manager. This new position required meticulous attention to detail, as I was responsible for several critical tasks:

- Receiving applications from customers interested in obtaining store credit. The application form required personal information such as name, address, employment details, and financial information.

- Reviewing applications for completeness and accuracy.

- Conducting a thorough credit check, verifying the applicant's credit history and score through credit bureaus.

- Explaining the credit acceptance process to the applicants. This included detailing how their creditworthiness was assessed and what factors influenced the decision.

- Explaining the credit terms, including the credit limit, interest rates, and repayment term.

- Communicating the reasons for the denial to the applicant. This required sensitivity and clarity, as it often involved discussing financial shortcomings or credit issues.

- Managing reports of lost or stolen credit cards, ensuring that these were processed promptly to prevent unauthorized use.

- Dealing with irate customers, using my communication skills to keep them calm and resolve their issues effectively. Handling difficult customers, while challenging, often lead to a deeper sense of job satisfaction. It provided an opportunity to turn a negative situation into a positive one, not just for the customer but for myself as well. Successfully navigating these interactions left me with a feeling of accomplishment and a reaffirmation of my problem-solving skills.

This role required a thorough understanding of the credit process, effective communication skills, and the ability to remain composed under pressure when dealing with upset customers. Most importantly, it demanded attention to detail, which was essential for maintaining accuracy and ensuring customer satisfaction. It was a significant step in my career, providing me with valuable experience in customer service and credit management.

These experiences contributed to my personal growth. They taught patience, empathy, and the ability to maintain composure under pressure—qualities that are invaluable in any professional setting. Each resolved conflict boost confidence in my abilities and reinforce the significance of my role in the industry.

In 1976, my passion for singing led me to join a gospel group where I sang with my friend Gwen for several years. It balanced my part-time and full-time jobs. One of the highlights of my time with the group was performing as the opening act for the legendary gospel singer Andraé Crouch at Constitution Hall in Washington, D.C. It was a momentous occasion that I will never forget.

By 1977 I had progressed from a GS 2 Clerk-Typist to a Secretary GS-5. I reached the height of my position in the office at NIH. I had a choice to either stay at the level that I was permanently, or transfer to another office or federal government agency and continue climbing the career ladder. I was ambitious and an opportunity to transfer to HEW - Public Health Service in Rockville, Maryland, opened as a Secretary GS-5. I stepped out on faith and accepted the position.

The position was located in the Division of Human Resources Planning and Development, Office of Administrative Management. The office was responsible for developing policies and programs in the areas of training, career planning, human resources development, staffing and recruitment. In my role as secretary to the Deputy Director, I screened all incoming mail to determine content, importance, and priority. I maintained correspondence control, indicating date received, to whom referred, deadlines for reply, and action required. I used this information for follow-up with all staff members. Routine mail was answered on my own initiative. I reviewed correspondence of all staff members for editorial accuracy as well as for completeness and conformity with Division policies and procedures. I kept up with and informed supervisors of any changes in correspondence, clearance procedures, and other policies and procedures.

I established and coordinated the maintenance of a variety of files and records for the Division, including the Federal Personnel Manual, and Administration Manuals.

I monitored telephone calls and followed up to assure that commitments made were kept. I was responsible for making appointments for my supervisor without prior clearance. I determined urgency of the problem in relation to demands placed on the supervisor's schedule. I tactfully handled all visitors to the office to determine which member of staff could provide the required assistance. I arranged for conferences on request, making sure that all interested people were notified, and that appropriate information was furnished either beforehand or at the time of the conference.

I prepared travel arrangements, obtained materials for attendance at outside conferences and conventions, prepared time and leave records, and purchased supplies and equipment as needed.

In September 1978, I made a significant career move by transferring from my position with the HEW in Maryland to accept a promotion at HEW in Washington, D.C., for a GS-6 Clerical Assistant at the Administration on Aging (AoA) in the immediate office of the Commissioner in S.W. Washington, D.C. This meant commuting from my suburban home in Rockville, Maryland into the busy city of D.C. I was willing to commute since I was getting a promotion and increase in pay.

This move was both exciting and daunting, as it meant leaving behind the familiar and stepping into a new environment. The promotion was a testament to my hard work and dedication, but it also required me to resign from my part-time evening job at the Hecht

Company department store where I enjoyed the work and the twenty percent off benefit that I used to purchase my clothes for work. The commute back to Maryland for the part time work was not feasible.

Career advancement opportunities were greater in D.C. than in Maryland. It was worth it to move where opportunities were promising. As a Clerical Assistant GS-6, I received visitors and telephone calls. I referred only essential visitors and callers to the Commissioner and Deputy Commissioner, and referred all others to appropriate offices in AoA or elsewhere (State or Area agencies, other Federal agencies, and private organizations). It was essential that I protect the already heavily loaded schedule of the Commissioner and Deputy Commissioner from non-essential additions; this had to be done quickly, but with great tact and discretion, since many of the callers/visitors held important positions in the Federal, State, and local governments, private industry, or national private organizations.

I was responsible for receiving, reviewing and distributing incoming correspondence; screened correspondence to refer non-essential items to the offices of AoA or elsewhere; and used the same knowledge as in screening visitors and callers.

I explained to visitors/callers about the AoA's activities and policies; I arranged travel and notified involved people; processed and reviewed incoming and outgoing written materials; maintained files; drafted letters/memos based on established information or verbal instructions; typed from handwritten drafts and assembled appropriate enclosures.

The nature of both reception and secretarial duties for the immediate office of a major federal program required that I use initiative to a significant degree in contacts with important officials inside and outside of the federal government.

To enhance my writing skills, my supervisor approved my request to take a job-relate course in English Composition from the University of the District of Columbia. I completed my course and it was my first college course that sparked my interest to get a college degree.

However, I could not afford college tuition and my employer would only pay for job-related courses. Consequently, I had to put college on hold, as I needed to continue working anyway.

Determined to maintain my financial stability, I began searching for a part-time evening job closer to my new full-time position in downtown D.C. I felt a mix of anticipation and anxiety as I navigated this transition, eager to prove myself in my new role while also ensuring I could support myself and help Mom out financially.

I found an opportunity to work part-time evenings at Raven Systems and Research, Inc., an information and computer systems development company that managed operations for several federal agencies. Accepting the word processor position there brought a sense of relief and renewed purpose. My role involved typing various contracts and processing data for federal agencies, tasks that required precision and efficiency. I prepared numerous documents, including correspondence, form letters, and reports, often under tight deadlines. The pressure was intense, but my background as a clerk-typist had equipped me well for these challenges.

Despite the demands, I felt a deep sense of accomplishment in my work. Each document I completed was a testament to my resilience and ability to adapt. This experience not only supplemented my income but also reinforced my belief in my capabilities and my commitment to personal and professional growth.

In 1980, I made a federal agency transition from HEW to the U.S. Department of the Interior, specifically to the Office of the Secretary of the Interior, Office of Small and Disadvantaged Business Utilization. This office was responsible for developing and implementing departmental programs for small and disadvantaged businesses and labor surplus areas. I applied for and secured a position as an Administrative Management Assistant, which elevated my clerical category and introduced me to new responsibilities and challenges. This promotion advanced me to a GS-7, with the potential to reach a GS-11.

As an Administrative Management Assistant, I took on a variety of liaison functions in areas such as personnel, procurement, payroll, printing and duplication, equipment maintenance and repair, transportation, training, and communication. My specific duties included coordinating and processing purchase requests, preparing justifications for purchases of goods and services, and arranging for maintenance, repairs, and training on all equipment. I meticulously maintained records on obligations and expenditures for all purchases and initiated personnel action requests for separations and recruitments.

I prepared semi-annual budget forecasting reports and maintained weekly commitment and obligation records for various budget object classes, including travel, personnel, employee benefits, printing and reproductions, supplies and materials, equipment, transportation of things, rent, communications, and utilities. I also secured office space and arranged for related services such as decorations, furnishings, and moving requirements. Keeping up-to-date floor plans and recommending better utilization of space were part of my responsibilities. I established and maintained office procedures for the acquisition, annual accountability, and disposal of office property.

In my role, I supervised the processing of travel arrangements for the Director and immediate staff, including schedules, authorizations, itineraries, and hotel reservations. I ensured that fiscal services received all travel authorizations in time to take advantage of discount airline fares, thereby stretching limited travel funds further.

I provided technical supervision to all clerical staff, offering orientation and training to new clerical and secretarial staff on established office policies and procedures. I reassigned and shifted clerical workloads as needed to meet special or fluctuating requirements. I prepared all correspondence regarding office space, property, procurement, and most personnel matters.

Additionally, I developed an effective correspondence control and tracking system for the clerical staff's daily operations.

I managed my supervisor's calendar, scheduling appointments without prior approval, and set priorities based on previous commitments. I prepared correspondence for my supervisor's signature on administrative matters such as office space, budget, procurement, and travel. I developed administrative guidelines, distributed copies to each secretary and clerk-typist, and periodically updated procedures and provided guidance as needed. I ensured that workload distribution was carried out in a manner most beneficial to the office. My supervisor was very pleased with my work, and I received a promotion to a GS-9.

In 1980, I attended an event at Zion Baptist Church in Washington, D.C., and later became a member. I shared my knowledge as a Sunday school teacher. My love for information sharing and helping others found a home there, and I cherished every moment spent in service. The Culture Club at Zion was a special ministry that brought joy and friendship, allowing us to explore and celebrate cultural activities together. As I reflect on these cherished memories, I am filled with gratitude for the fellowship and growth that Zion provided during my time there.

Another significant time in my life that gave me joy was on June 12, 1982, when I had a change of heart about marriage. I married a man I had dated for 7 years. I had reservations about getting married for so long because of the experiences that my Mom went through living in a dysfunctional home. However, my husband is just what I needed — someone who could be encouraging and supportive of my ambitions.

In 1983, after more than ten years of advancing in my federal career, just when everything was going well for me, I resigned from the U.S. Department of Labor because of a personal situation. This moment was one of the most challenging periods of my life. Leaving a career I had worked so hard to build was devastating. The sense of loss was profound, as my work had become a significant part of my identity and daily routine.

The impact of my resignation was multifaceted. Professionally, it meant stepping away from a role where I had grown and thrived, leaving behind colleagues and a work environment that had become like a second family. The responsibilities I had taken on, the long hours I had worked on Saturday mornings to accomplish my tasks and meet deadlines that no one knew, the daily working lunch breaks I had at my desk, the skills I had improved, and the progress I had made were all put on hold. It felt like hitting the pause button on a journey that had been steadily moving forward.

Personally, the resignation brought about a period of introspection and reevaluation. It was a time to reassess my priorities and consider what truly mattered to me. The decision to resign, though difficult and regretful, was necessary for my personal well-being. It was a reminder that sometimes, life requires us to make tough choices and that our careers, while important, are just one aspect of our lives.

My loving, understanding husband, helped me recognize that this experience was an invaluable lesson about resilience and adaptability. It reinforced the idea that setbacks are a natural part of life and that it's essential to rise again after falling. This period of my life became a testament to my ability to navigate through adversity and emerge stronger.

Ultimately, my resignation was not the end of my journey but a pivotal moment that shaped my future. It allowed me to refocus, and eventually return to the workforce with renewed vigor and a deeper understanding of my strengths and values. This experience underscored the importance of perseverance and the belief that every setback is an opportunity for growth.

Between 1983 and 1984, during my break from federal government service, I had an assortment of jobs — searching for satisfaction and pay increase. I accepted a secretarial position at Tracor, Inc., a defense electronics contractor in Rockville, Maryland. This role involved managing the office to ensure efficient operations. I provided general secretarial services for six professional staff members. I was responsible for typing correspondence, memos, reports and statistical tables, maintaining filing systems, answering phones, taking messages, and directing calls to the appropriate staff. I also scheduled appointments, updated my supervisor's event calendar, arranged staff meetings, and managed incoming and outgoing mail. This role required decision-making, interpersonal, and organizational skills, as well as basic writing skills for brief memos, all of which I had perfected in previous secretarial and administrative positions.

After resigning from the Department of Interior and returning to Maryland, I had to leave my part-time evening job at Raven Research Systems, Inc. in D.C. Although my husband could support me, I was accustomed to working two jobs and valued my independence. I found a job at Bob's Big Boy Restaurant in Rockville, conveniently located near my full-time job at Tracor, Inc.

As a hostess and waitress assistant, I welcomed customers, escorted them to their tables, assured them their server would be with them shortly, and took reservations. On busy days, I assisted wherever needed — clearing tables and ensuring tables were properly set. This role required good communication skills, decision-making, and adaptability.

Although I was unhappy with the pay at the restaurant, I embraced the lessons and skills it offered. After one evening of standing for hours, I knew I wouldn't last long at this job. However, I persevered. This job, unlike others, made me very tired after working a full-time job. Every night, my feet burned and ached. I will never forget every night my husband soaked and massaged my feet. I appreciated it, but I was determined to find another part-time evening job.

In the spring of 1983, I secured a part-time evening job at Com Print, a small local newspaper company in Gaithersburg, Maryland. I received on-the-job training and was responsible for receiving ads and various information to typeset and prepare for printing in the weekly newspaper. Working under pressure and meeting tight deadlines were major requirements. I learned to typeset using various fonts, design and create graphics, and layout involving margins, columns, spacing, headers, and footers. While this was an interesting job and a new skill to add to my experiences, after a few months, I decided to pursue something that interested me more.

In the summer of 1983, I took on a part-time evening role as a Cash Office Associate at Lord and Taylor's Department Store in the White Flint Mall, in Kensington, Maryland. Lord and Taylor was renowned for its high-quality and fashionable retail offerings, including clothing, accessories, jewelry, beauty products, and home goods. This position was a significant shift from my previous roles, providing a unique set of challenges and learning opportunities.

As a Cash Office Associate, my primary responsibility was to manage the cash flow within the store. Throughout the evening, sales associates would bring periodic cash deposits to the office. My role involved meticulously confirming the amounts turned in while the sales associate observed, ensuring there were no discrepancies. This process required a high level of integrity and attention to detail, as any errors could lead to significant financial discrepancies.

At the close of business each day, I logged all cash deposits, ensuring that the records were accurate and up-to-date. This task demanded strong organizational skills and a methodical approach to ensure that all transactions were accounted for correctly. Confidentiality was paramount in this role, as I handled large sums of money and sensitive financial information.

Working in the cash office also required excellent teamwork. I collaborated closely with other associates and supervisors to ensure smooth operations, especially during the busy holiday season. Effective communication was essential to coordinate the flow of cash and address any issues that arose promptly.

My role at Lord and Taylor taught me the importance of precision and reliability in financial management. It also reinforced the value of integrity and confidentiality in handling sensitive information. Despite the challenges, I appreciated the opportunity to develop new skills and contribute to the store's operations during one of the busiest times of the year.

During the holiday season of 1983, I seized the opportunity to work part-time evenings and weekends at I. Magnin, a high-end retailer renowned for its luxury goods and fashion at the same mall as Lord and Taylor. I. Magnin offered an array of designer clothing, footwear, jewelry, and beauty products. While working at Lord and Taylor, I often spent my breaks wandering through I. Magnin, captivated by the elegance and sophistication of its merchandise. It was a step above Lord and Taylor, and I felt as though I belonged there.

Driven by this aspiration, I resigned from Lord and Taylor and joined I. Magnin's credit office. In this role, I assisted the credit manager with various tasks, similar to those I had performed at the Hecht Company and Lord and Taylor, including processing credit applications, managing customer accounts, and handling billing inquiries. I also ensured accurate record-keeping and provided exceptional customer service to clients. The skills and lessons I had acquired from my previous roles prepared me well for this position, allowing me to seamlessly transition into my new responsibilities at I. Magnin.

This experience was pivotal in my career growth. It not only enhanced my skills in credit management and customer service but also exposed me to a higher standard of retail operations. The professionalism and attention to detail required at I. Magnin elevated my work ethic and broadened my understanding of luxury retail. These lessons and skills became invaluable as I progressed in my career, laying a strong foundation for future roles and responsibilities.

On a personal level, this period marked significant growth. Working at I. Magnin instilled in me a deeper sense of confidence and ambition. It taught me the value of pursuing my aspirations and stepping out of my comfort zone. The challenges I faced and overcame during this time strengthened my resilience and adaptability, qualities that have been instrumental throughout my career. These lessons and skills became invaluable as I progressed in my career, laying a strong foundation for future roles and responsibilities.

Each day, as I balanced the demands of my full-time job with my part-time role at this elegant store, I absorbed lessons not listed in any employee handbook. The art of fashion became my silent tutor, teaching me the language of lines and patterns.

To this day, the qualities of I. Magnin resonate in my every choice of attire, especially when I dress for church. Everything matches; hat, clothes, shoes, and purse. Dressing well is not a mere act of vanity; it is a tribute to the elegance that once schooled me, a daily homage to the beauty of order and the power of presentation. It is a testament to the truth that, no matter our origins, we can all choose to wear dignity and grace.

My experience working part-time evenings and week-ends at I. Magnin department store had a lasting impact on my appreciation for fashion and style. Such experience has influenced my sense of elegance and professionalism. This aspect of my journey shows the multifaceted nature of my personal growth. It's not just about career advancement but also about the development of personal tastes and the refinement of my own style.

One day, during a casual conversation, I shared a glimpse of my past with a colleague. Their eyes widened in disbelief. "I can't imagine you working on a farm," they said. "You don't look like you've had hard times."

It was in that moment I realized how much my story differed from the assumptions people made based on my appearance. People often see the success, achievements, or positive aspects of someone's life without understanding the struggles, challenges, and hard work that went into reaching that point. To this day, people often compliment me on my polished appearance and articulate speech, assuming I came from a prominent family. For this reason, some were even jealous of me, but little do they know, my journey was paved with challenges, perseverance, and hard work that brought me to where I am today. This is a perfect example of the saying, "You see my glory but you don't know my story," and "You can't judge a book by its cover."

In February 1984, I embarked on another full-time job with Info-Disc Corporation, a small, private, innovative information technology service company based in Gaithersburg, Maryland. This company specialized in making college information accessible on discs, a cutting-edge solution at the time. As the Administrative Assistant to both the President and Vice President of this growing company, my responsibilities were vast and varied. I was tasked with organizing and managing the office, establishing comprehensive office procedures, and creating an extensive filing system. My role also involved preparing correspondence, interfacing with clients, assigning clients to sales representatives, and ensuring their workloads ran smoothly. Additionally, I handled the procurement of office supplies and materials, responded to phone calls and messages, arranged meetings, and supervised mass mailings.

The skills required for these tasks were multifaceted. I needed to be highly organized, capable of working well under pressure, and adept at both independent and team-based work.

Meeting tight deadlines and communicating effectively were also crucial to my success in this role. However, the challenges were significant. As a newly developed company, Info-Disc required me to navigate uncharted waters, often without a clear roadmap. Balancing the demands of a growing business while establishing foundational processes was a test of my resilience and adaptability.

By August of 1984, a more secured opportunity presented itself. I was offered a full-time position at Westat Survey Research, Inc. in Rockville, Maryland, a company renowned for its research and information services. As a Research Administrative Assistant at Westat, my duties expanded further. Collaborating closely with the project manager, I developed agendas, scheduled meetings, prepared and distributed meeting materials, and managed meeting distribution lists. I also drafted, finalized, and distributed meeting summaries. My role included performing data entry, conducting quality control checks, engaging in telephone data collection, drafting and maintaining work instructions, study procedures, and other essential study materials.

The skills I practiced at Westat were invaluable. Effective communication, self-motivation, organization, attention to detail, and the ability to work well both independently and within a team were essential. Additionally, I learned to convey the purpose and importance of our studies to respondents, ensuring their understanding and cooperation. Adapting to a different organizational culture and mastering new responsibilities required perseverance and a willingness to continuously learn and grow.

After two months of working at Westat, I received a call from the U.S. Department of Labor in Washington, D.C., to come in for an interview for a Secretary GS-4 position. I had waited over a year for this call. Although I was overqualified for the position, I accepted the job because I wanted to be reinstated to federal government. I was determined to work my way back up the career ladder. This determination paid off, as I successfully navigated my way through the grades, proving that perseverance and dedication can indeed lead to achieving one's goals.

On October 28, 1984, I was reinstated to federal government and accepted the downgraded GS-4 Secretary position with the U.S. Department of Labor, Employment and Training Administration (ETA), Office of Strategic Planning Policy and Development. I resigned my full-time position at Westat and my part-time-evening job at I. Magnin to commute to D.C. to get my career back on track. The role I accepted turned out to be a blessing, offering me better advancement opportunities that eventually led to a GS-13 position with a six-figure salary. As my pastor would say, "My setback was a setup for a comeback," reminding me of the classic saying, "When one door closes, another opens."

Determined to prove my qualifications and capabilities, I worked diligently, adhering to the work ethic instilled in me since childhood—long hours, early starts, no breaks, and late nights to meet deadlines. I also volunteered to assist the professional staff with projects, demonstrating my ability to perform at a higher level. My supervisor was so pleased with my performance that he often remarked, "She can walk on water." His humorous comment not only made us laugh but also placed me on a pedestal, motivating me to never let him down.

As a secretary, my responsibilities included receiving telephone inquiries and personal visitors, ascertaining the nature of their business, handling requests personally when possible, and referring others to the appropriate staff. I maintained control records on incoming and outgoing correspondence, followed up on items with due dates, and ensured routine correspondence was responded to in a timely manner. I made all travel arrangements for my supervisor and staff members, including preparing itineraries and typing travel vouchers upon their return.

I typed a variety of materials from rough handwritten drafts and brief oral instructions, including letters, memoranda, reports, and guides. I managed time and attendance records, maintained the office filing system, and established and deleted files as necessary. Additionally, I maintained my supervisor's appointment calendar, prioritizing appointments based on established priorities. I served as a liaison between the Unit Chief and subordinate staff members, coordinating clerical functions with other clerical personnel. Each year, I received outstanding performance appraisals. Within two years, I was promoted to a GS-6.

In April 1987, my supervisor received a promotion and he transferred to ETA's Office of Job Training Programs, as the New Division Chief for Program Development and Interpretation. When he learned there was a staff assistant position opening in ETA, Office of Employment Security Unemployment Insurance Service (UIS) in the Director's office, he recommended me and I was hired with a promotion of GS-7 working with the Director's Executive Assistant.

As a staff assistant, I prepared all personnel action requests for the UIS Division of the ETA. This included handling resignations, retirements, details, reassignments, vacancy recruitment requests, promotions, and name changes. I served as the staff-level liaison with the Office of Personnel on related matters and established a secure, accurate, and up-to-date system of personnel records.

One of my notable achievements was streamlining the personnel records system, which significantly improved the efficiency and accuracy of our record-keeping processes. This initiative led to a more organized and accessible database.

I maintained the UIS correspondence control system for all controlled correspondence and action documents. My responsibilities included reviewing all outgoing memos and letters prepared for the Director's signature. I regularly reminded staff of controlled correspondence due dates and diplomatically followed up on their status until completion. Additionally, I typed memoranda, letters, and reports, and assisted in preparing various regular and special reports, including personnel status reports and EEO accomplishment reports.

I also prepared responses to miscellaneous requests from administrative services, covering telephones, space, equipment inventories, and usage. I received, tracked, and independently resolved UIS administrative service requests and complaints, including equipment maintenance and repairs, and facilities maintenance issues.

During the spring and fall semesters, I decided to go back to college for a few more courses. For job enhancement and career development, my supervisor approved my request to take 3 job-related college courses from Montgomery College in Rockville, Maryland: Personnel Management, Technical Writing, and Introduction to Business.

Teamwork, the ability to work under pressure, organizational skills, and communication skills were crucial for success in my position. My efforts were consistently recognized with highly effective performance appraisals.

In January of 1987, I was invited to form a partnership with four friends to create a small home-based catering business on weekends. At the time, I had no part-time job to supplement my income, so the opportunity came at the perfect moment, and I eagerly agreed to the partnership. I have always been interested in trying new jobs and learning new skills, so I embraced this new venture. I wanted to be well-rounded and knowledgeable in more than one profession, ensuring I had other skills to fall back on if needed. This mindset was influenced by my parents, who had no transferable skills and were confined to farm and domestic work.

Catering required hard work and commitment, which came naturally to me. As a member of the catering team, we provided services for weddings, corporate events, and social gatherings. We handled everything from food preparation to distribution. While working in the kitchen and preparing food was enjoyable at times, it could also be challenging, especially when catering for large groups. We prided ourselves on offering a variety of foods that were not only visually appealing but also delicious and consistently pleasing our customers.

Once a budget was determined, we created a menu based on the customer's budget, finalized head counts and menu items, and shopped for the necessary ingredients. We transported food and other items to the venue, set up and decorated the buffet tables, managed event schedules, and adhered to food preparation timelines. After the event, we cleaned up and ensured no items were left behind. The role of a caterer required effective teamwork, excellent organizational and communication skills, patience, and cooking expertise. I had developed these skills through various jobs and experiences from my childhood, which prepared me well to achieve the goals of our catering business.

In February of 1987, a new opportunity emerged. The Department of Labor introduced a Management Intern Program (MIP) to select and develop five high-potential GS-5 and GS-7 employees and outside candidates for rotational work assignments. This career development program aimed to train future leaders and managers within the federal government, providing valuable on-the-job

training and experience for Manpower Development Specialists (later renamed Workforce Development Specialists). The program offered yearly promotions from GS-5 to GS-12, contingent on quality work performance.

The MIP was managed by the ETA's Office of Job Training Programs, Division of Program Development and Interpretation, where my former supervisor had been transferred. Remembering my quality work, professional potential, and work ethic, he encouraged me to apply for one of the MIP positions. The GS-7 and GS-9 positions required a college degree and a one-year MIP, while the GS-5 position accepted experience with a two-year MIP. Lacking a degree, I accepted the GS-5 position, which was a downgrade. However, it was in a professional category, and my salary remained equivalent to my GS-7 grade level. I was willing to take a step back to advance, believing I had more to gain with yearly promotions to GS-12. This opportunity would not have been possible in Clerical, Secretarial, or Staff Assistance positions, which do not offer such high grades. I was honored by my former supervisor's belief in me.

I transferred to the MIP office and began my two-year Workforce Development Specialist MIP. It started with a 30-day rotational assignment at the Department of Labor's Regional Offices in Chicago, Illinois, where I learned about regional program operations, the collaboration between regional offices and states, and the connection between regional and National Office responsibilities under the Job Training Partnership Act (JTPA).

As a Workforce Development Specialist, I achieved several significant accomplishments:

- Provided program information, advice, and guidance through telephone contacts and correspondence on the interpretation and implementation of established JTPA policies and procedures.

- Developed ETA Issuances on policies and procedures concerning JTPA and related programs, and drafted regulations to implement portions of the proposed Worker Readjustment Program.

- Reviewed JTPA national reserve project proposals submitted by the states for programmatic content and compliance review guides from Regional Offices for accuracy and completeness. My thorough reviews ensured that projects met all necessary criteria and standards.

- Designed and developed employment and training program requirements through regulations, policy interpretations, and other directives for special programs authorized by congressional and other authorities. My contributions helped shape the framework for these programs, ensuring they were effective and compliant with legislative mandates.

- Provided information and clarification on policies by responding to inquiries from Congress, other governmental agencies, private organizations, and the public. My ability to communicate complex policies clearly and effectively was instrumental in maintaining transparency and understanding.

- Researched, developed, and provided National Office reports and recommendations, offering input into alternatives and options regarding the national budget for submission to the Office of Management and Budget. My insights and recommendations were crucial in shaping budgetary decisions.

- Developed procedures and guidelines for state applications for dislocated worker funds, reviewed and made recommendations on state proposals, notified states of review results, and developed grant packages for accepted proposals. My work ensured that states received the necessary funding to support dislocated workers effectively.

- Developed procedures and guidelines for appeals under the JTPA designation and local job training plan. My efforts ensured that the appeals process was fair, transparent, and accessible.

- Participated in meetings and conferences impacting employment and training programs, where I provided valuable insights and contributed to strategic discussions. My participation helped shape the direction of these programs.

- Prepared comprehensive briefing reports for executive staff, ensuring they were well-informed and equipped to make strategic decisions.

By 1989, my interest in my part-time catering business began to decrease. However, I found great satisfaction in my full-time job and felt blessed to be back working for the federal government. That year, Mom's health deteriorated, and on Christmas Eve, she passed away. I was devastated, feeling as though I had lost a part of myself. Reflecting on the many sacrifices she made for me and my efforts to care for her as a young teen, I was deeply moved when I heard her say to  her siblings, who were standing by her bed side, "God is going to bless Ceola because she was the only child that stuck by me."

I responded, "I didn't do it for a blessing, mom, I did it because you're my mother and I love you." My mother always encouraged me to do well with my life, and kept me in her prayers, I miss her every day. Her wise words of wisdom and prayers are always with me.

After two weeks of leave for the funeral and handling my mother's personal affairs, I immersed myself in work, pushing harder than ever. While this helped me get through the days, the nights were difficult. My mind often wandered, thinking of my mom and missing her terribly. I dreamt of her frequently and looked forward to sleep just to see her in my dreams. The pain was profound, and I struggled to find solace. I knew mom would not want me worrying myself sick. I realized I needed something beyond work to occupy my mind and bring fulfillment. I decided to take up a hobby. I love flowers so I thought I would try my hand in silk floral designing. I took several informal classes in flower arranging, purchased various quality silk flowers, and studied floral design books, videos, and magazines. I practiced on my own and even took my floral design books with me on business trips, studying in my hotel room at night.

Floral design became my hobby, providing both enjoyment and therapy. It was so relaxing that I would come home from my full-time job and create numerous silk arrangements. After about six months, I wanted to expand my knowledge and learn the flower shop business. I mustered the courage to volunteer at a local flower shop a couple of nights a week. There, I received on-the-job training, learning to care for and design fresh flowers, take customer orders, and create window displays with silk flowers. I learned quickly and worked hard. I did so well that after a few weeks, they offered me a paying part-time evening and weekend job.

Taking my interest further, I joined several floral designer networking organizations, attended floral design workshops, seminars, and numerous bridal and craft shows to learn as much as I could about the flower industry. I resigned from the part-time catering business partnership to focus more on the flower industry. My hobby became my part-time job.

By the end of 1990, I felt confident enough to start my own small home-based business designing silk and fresh flower arrangements. I obtained a retail sales tax license and created marketing tools such as business cards, brochures, and flyers. I set up table displays at bridal and craft shows in hotels, community centers, and event companies hosting wedding vendor shows. I designed everything from holiday wreaths to wedding bouquets and table centerpieces. I even arranged for one of the bridal show coordinators to have their model brides carry my floral bouquets as part of the advertising. From this show alone, I received numerous orders for spring and fall weddings.

After a year in business, I wanted to learn how to be a wedding coordinator and consultant. I joined the Association of Wedding Coordinators and Bridal Consultants, a local networking organization that provides workshops, seminars, support, assistance, and educational opportunities. This organization promotes and encourages the highest level of ethics and professionalism in the wedding industry. After a few months of studying and learning a new skill, I expanded my business to include a wide range of special event services—wedding consultation and coordination, social, residential, and commercial event planning and management. I changed my business name to reflect a complete package of wedding and special event services, and it proved to be effective for my business and brought many more customers.

Most of my customers came from word of mouth and seeing my work firsthand at events I serviced. I recall one wedding in particular where I provided floral designs and wedding day coordination. I ensured the wedding day schedule of events was seamless and timely, from early arrival to decorating the church, distributing flowers to the wedding party, and getting them down the aisle in time for the ceremony. I also decorated the reception venue and ensured the photographer, baker, musicians, and other service providers arrived on time. As a result of seeing my service, two of the bridesmaids, who were engaged to be married, requested my services to plan and manage their weddings. I gained these customers from doing one wedding. This job required patience, attention to detail, the ability to work under pressure, reliability, dedication, and a pleasant personality. All of which I learned from previous jobs.

My hobby turned into a lucrative, steady part-time job for 15 years until I went back to college. At that point, I had to let the business go to focus on getting my degree. With the support of my husband, who helped with deliveries, equipment setup, decorations, cleanup, and everything I needed, I achieved my goal of owning and operating a small but quality home-based special event business.

In 1991, I progressed to a GS-12 position, taking on additional work assignments, including managing numerous demonstration grants. As a Grants and Contracts Specialist, I planned and managed webinars, created and updated office standard operating procedures, and provided project management for numerous Dislocated Workers Demonstration Grant Programs. I reviewed and recommended approval of grant applications up to ten million dollars, planned conferences and grant award events, and arranged hotel accommodations, speakers, and transportation to ensure a smooth flow of activities. I reviewed and analyzed grantee and contractor progress and financial expenditure reports, traveled to various states to conduct on-site grant project monitoring, and prepared comprehensive reports of my findings. I also reviewed, certified, and approved contractor invoices for payment, conducted presentations to foreign dignitaries on policy and employment and training programs, wrote correspondence on employment and training services, contracts, and grant issues, and conducted interviews for Intergovernmental Personnel Agreements and negotiated contracts.

Among a team of demonstration grants and contract managers, I was the only African American female GS-12, while the other five were Caucasian men and women at the GS-13 level. Despite performing the same duties and consistently receiving annual performance appraisals of highly effective and outstanding, I was never promoted to GS-13. Although I felt intimidated because my colleagues had degrees and I did not. Despite the challenges, I maintained high performance to prevent any negative evaluations.

In 1994, a new Office Director assigned me additional responsibilities previously managed by a GS-15 Office Director who had resigned. I had assisted him with providing policy guidance on the WARN Act, making me the obvious choice to continue that role. I managed the WARN Act effectively along with my other duties and responsibilities, consistently receiving annual performance appraisals of highly effective and outstanding. Despite my increased workload and demonstrated capabilities, I was never promoted to a GS-13. Nevertheless, I possessed all the qualities required for my job and continued to excel in my role.

Throughout this period, my resilience was my greatest asset. Despite facing potential discrimination and feeling intimidated by my colleagues' educational backgrounds, I remained steadfast in my commitment to excellence. I balanced a demanding workload, pursued my degree, and continued to deliver quality performance. My resilience not only helped me navigate these challenges but also reinforced my belief in my capabilities and potential for growth.

The WARN Act is an employment law that, with certain exceptions, requires employers with at least 100 employees to provide advance written notice of layoffs and business closings. WARN Act is a critical piece of legislation that provides workers with important protections during times of significant employment changes. My role in advising on the WARN Act was vital in ensuring that both employers and employees understand their rights and responsibilities.

Specifically, as an Employment Law Advisor, I analyzed and explained the WARN law and regulations, developed layoff compliance assistance material, and advised congressional officials, attorneys, employers, workers, and media on layoff law requirements via written and verbal communication. Provided presentations, conducted research on nationwide layoffs and provided written reports. I provided leadership in training and policy projects to five team members.

My ability to respond to inquiries from senators, congressional representatives, employers and employees, demonstrated the trust placed in my expertise. My work has had a meaningful impact on the lives of many individuals affected by layoffs and plant closings. I found this aspect of my work rewarding and it speaks volumes about my dedication to public service.

My career progression from clerical work to an advisory role highlights my adaptability, continuous learning, and commitment to excellence. These qualities contributed to my success in providing guidance on employment law.

The diverse skills that I acquired throughout my career seamlessly translated into my role within the federal government. These skills have not only contributed to my success in the federal government but have also enabled me to approach challenges with a well-rounded perspective that made me an effective and respected WARN Act Policy/ Employment Law Advisor.

The journey to a GS-13 level within the federal government was a testament to perseverance in the face of systemic barriers. Despite my extensive experience and partial college education, my applications for GS-13 positions were met with a consistent refrain in rejection letters: "Although you are qualified and have the experience, you lack the education required for the position." This message underscored the necessity of a degree, a credential I was working towards but had not yet secured.

Determined to overcome this obstacle, I resolved to complete my degree and ensure that my qualifications would be unquestionable. However, the path to advancement was further complicated by the practice of preselection. Many internal positions I wanted were open for application, yet the outcomes were predetermined, favoring preselected candidates. This process rendered our efforts pointless, degree or not.

A particularly disheartening episode occurred when I competed for a GS-13 role advertised within my own department. Despite my intimate knowledge of the responsibilities and my proven track record, the position was awarded to an external candidate. The following year brought organizational changes, and my role as Employment Law Advisor was scheduled for relocation. The manager of the receiving office, recognizing my expertise, extended an offer for me to transition alongside my position, coupled with the long-awaited promotion to GS-13.

Confronted with a choice between loyalty to my current office and the advancement of my career, I engaged in a candid discussion with my existing manager. I reminded him when he had the opportunity to promote me, he hired the external candidate. I expressed the negative impact his decision had on me. He expressed regret for his past decisions and offered me a potential promotion should I remain. He confided that previous opportunities for my advancement had been thwarted by his supervisors, favoring external connections with personal friends over internal employee merit. He also said that if I told anyone he would deny it. Of course I never did tell, but I've carried that with me for years. It is pre-selection situations like this that has held me and others back from promotions we earned and deserved. His admission, though offered in confidence, did little to change the years of professional setbacks and personal disappointment.

Ultimately, the decision was clear. My commitment to my work as the WARN Act Policy/Employment Law Advisor and the recognition of my proficiency by the new office solidified my choice. I accepted the move, embracing the promotion to GS-13 and the end of years of dedication. It was a touching moment of validation and a significant milestone in my career. Later, my former supervisor was reassigned and his position was replaced. I suppose this is an example of what they say about Karma — it comes back on you. So it is best to be careful how you treat people, you don't know when you may need them again.

In my daily work as the WARN Act Policy/Employment Law Advisor, I diligently studied the WARN Act and its regulations, striving to perfect my understanding to provide effective policy guidance. Much of my training, however, is owed to Mr. Waxman, a lawyer in the Department of Labor's Solicitor's Office. Whenever I faced challenging telephone inquiries about WARN's requirements, I could always rely on Mr. Waxman's assistance. I am deeply grateful for the patience and time he invested in explaining and helping me better understand the WARN Act.

My role as demonstration grant project manager required frequent business travel. Initially, this was exciting, as it provided opportunities for professional and career development. I interacted with a diverse group of people, some who inspired me to engage in community service work, which I discuss in Chapter 5. My travel included the following cities and states:

Travel Dates	**City and State**	**Purpose**
Feb 28 – Mar 25, 1988	Chicago, IL	Rotational Training Assignment to learn DOL Regional Office Program Operations
Sept. 24 - 25, 1991	Columbus, OH	Job Training Partnership Act Management Information Systems Conference
June 23 -25, 1992	Kansas City, MO	Provide Rapid Response Training

Feb. 13 – 16, 1994	Charleston, SC	Defense Demonstration Grant Conference
May 2 – 3, 1994	Denver, CO	Provide Rapid Response Training
June 1 – 3, 1994	Chicago, IL	Provide Rapid Response Training
June 5 – 10, 1994	Boston, MA, Bangor, ME, Syracuse, NY	Monitor Defense Conversion Adjustment Assistance Demonstration Grant Project
Nov. 27 – Dec. 02, 1994	Austin, Dallas, Ft. Worth, TX	Monitor DCA Demo Grant Project Monitor DCA Demo Grant Project
April 4 – 6, 1996	Cincinnati, Ohio	Monitor Career Management Account Demonstration Grant Program Project
April 16, 1996	Manhattan, NY	CMA Demo Grant Program Project
May 21 – 24, 1996	Phoenix, Az	CMA Demo Grant Program Project
Sept. 23 – 26, 1996	Atlanta, GA	CMA Demo Grant Program Project
April 1 -- 3, 1997	Kansas City, MO	Provide National Reserve Account Training

July 27 – 29, 1998	New Orleans, LA	Monitor Truck Driver Trng. Demo Project
	Biloxi, MS	Monitor Truck Driver Trng. Demo Project
Sept. 27 -29, 1999	Nashville, TN	Monitor Truck Driver Trng. Demo Project
Jan 11 – Dec 12, 1999	Harrisburg, PA	Monitor Truck Driver Trng. Demo Project

CHAPTER 4

HARMONY IN DUAL ROLES: NAVIGATING MARRIAGE AND CAREER

While working at NIH, I met my husband at Vermont Avenue Baptist Church in 1975. We married in 1982, during my tenure at the Department of Interior. One Sunday morning, while seated on the main level at church, I noticed him in the balcony. He was attractive and well dressed. The following Sunday, I sat in the balcony behind him and struck up a conversation before the service began. He wore a fashionable dark two-piece suit and exquisite shoes. His appearance was classy, captivating, and impressive, aligning with my own reputation for stylish clothes and shoes. As time passed, we dated and got to know each other better. I learned that he was also federally employed, educated, established, and shared many of my values and interests, such as music, theater, travel, art museums, and performing arts. Despite our differences — he was quiet while I enjoyed conversation — we accepted each other as we were.

As I mentioned in Chapter 2, I never wanted to get married or have children due to my upbringing. However, after seven years of knowing my husband, I changed my mind about marriage, though I still did not want children. He had children from a previous marriage and graciously accepted my decision. We've been together for 49 years and married for 42 years. We did not need children to bond our marriage.

My humble beginnings and dysfunctional home made me very independent and career-minded. It was important to me to have someone supportive of my goals and beliefs, and, established, as I was. Despite our different backgrounds — I'm from the country, and he's from the city — our compatible values and interests made me believe he was the right person for me.

Communication has been the cornerstone of our relationship. From the very beginning, we made it a point to talk openly and honestly about our goals, dreams, and concerns. This mutual understanding and respect have been vital in navigating our dual roles in marriage and career. Some of the most memorable times when my husband was supportive of me include:

- **Part-time Jobs:** With all the part-time evening jobs that kept me out late, my husband never complained. He knew where I was, what I was doing, and what I wanted to achieve, because we communicated openly about our plans and aspirations.

- **Church Decorations:** For nine years, I served as the church decorator for Vermont Avenue Baptist Church. My husband was by my side helping with every decoration project. He even collected boxes and made custom-sized ones to carry items in. Also, at Canaan Baptist Church where we are currently members, he helped with church decorations. He hung numerous pictures and other artifacts, set up newly ordered banquet tables and chairs, and provided other handyman services. Our ability to communicate effectively ensured that we worked seamlessly together.

- **Floral Designs:** For fifteen years, I managed a part-time, home-based floral design and event planning business. My husband was always there, making deliveries, helping decorate, and assisting with whatever I needed. Our constant communication allowed us to coordinate and support each other efficiently.

- **College:** When I went back to college part-time while working full-time, my husband never complained. He even helped me with challenging math courses using his engineering skills. Our open communication about my academic challenges, and his willingness to help, made a significant difference.

- **Business Travel:** As a demonstration grants and contracts project manager at the Department of Labor, I had to travel for business several times a year. My husband never complained. When I was away in Chicago for a 30-day Management Intern Program assignment, he visited on weekends to spend time with me. Our regular communication kept us connected despite the distance.

- **Community Service Work:** When I joined several community service organizations and worked on fundraising events, my husband assisted with whatever I needed and supported the events financially by attending them. Our shared commitment and communication made these endeavors successful.

- **Commuting from Delaware to D.C.:** Five months before I retired, we moved to Delaware. My husband, already retired, drove me to the train station every day and picked me up without complaint, despite the six-hour round trip commute. Our daily communication about the logistics and our mutual support made this challenging period manageable.

- **College Graduation:** When it was time for my graduation from college, my husband was so supportive and proud that he thought of having a graduation luncheon celebration for me after the ceremony. Together we planned the venue, menu, and number of guests and he took care of all the expenses for my family and friends. His thoughtful and generous gift made the event special.

All that I was involved in, my husband could have demanded that I make other arrangements, but he never did. He was always there for me. He was my rock, and I deeply appreciate all of his support.

College graduation day was May 13, 2008. I completed all my course work. I earned a Bachelor of Science degree in Business Administration, and certifications in Management Foundations and Women in Business from the University of Maryland University College.

On May 17, before heading out to participate in my graduation ceremony, early that morning my husband and I reminisced and laughed about those times when we had to make time to spend together in between working, traveling, and studying. We did what we needed to do to accomplish the goals. We agreed that a little time together was better than no time at all.

Balancing marriage and a full-time career and other family responsibilities with the rigors of academia was no small achievement, but it taught me the value of time, the importance of setting priorities, and the strength that lies within.

Earning my degree was a symbol of my resilience, a beacon that guided me through uncertainty. As I look back on the winding road that led me here, I am still filled with gratitude for every challenge overcome and every lesson learned. I am thankful for the encouragement and understanding I received from my husband standing by my side every step of the way. This milestone is not just a testament to academic success, but a tribute to the spirit that propelled me forward through countless challenges.

Balancing work-life and marriage can be challenging. However, planning, time management, and multitasking were key in helping me successfully accomplish several responsibilities. Because my husband and I were understanding and supportive of each other's activities, I was able to balance my marriage and career in ways that were mutually beneficial. Before venturing out to do the things

I needed to do, I would get out of bed extra early to do housework and prepare meals for my husband. This way, when I wasn't at home, there were plenty of meals in the fridge for him to select from and just warm up.

When we planned an event, and I had course work, while he drove, I studied. If it was an out of town event, I took my books with me and studied after we spent time together. I also studied coursework while riding the subway to and from work, which was a two-hour round trip, and during lunch breaks or when my workload was slow. By the time I arrived home from work or class, my coursework was complete, and I had time to sit and spend time with my husband. There was never a time when work or personal life dominated the other because they were well-planned. Even while working full-time and part-time and studying

college work, I still made time as much as I could to be a wife, stepmother, sister, aunt, niece, friend, and helped anyone who asked. I learned multitasking and time management from the work ethics instilled in me from farm work. I believe in the old saying, "Where there is a will, there is a way." I had the will, and I made it happen. After 42 years, we still enjoy our personal interests and hobbies separately and together.

CHAPTER 5

COMMUNITY SERVICE: WHEN HELPING OTHERS BECOMES YOUR HOBBY

In my journey of community service, I have had the honor of being a member of several community service organizations. In 1996, during my business travel, I became friends with one of my regional colleagues who shared her community service work experience with the National Coalition of 100 Black Women (NCBW). I was so impressed that I decided to become a member of NCBW Montgomery County, Maryland Chapter. NCBW advocates on behalf of Black women and girls. NCBW provides leadership opportunities, role modeling, mentoring, and initiatives to improve academic achievement and increase levels of aspiration.

During my time with the organization, I co-chaired the planning of our annual scholarship events. I managed contract negotiations with venues, designed table decorations, managed printing of flyers, programs, tickets, handling public relations with celebrity guests, and coordinated with major fashion show sponsors and high-end furriers. Also, I served on the Youth Committee, where I scheduled weekly tutoring sessions with elementary and middle school students and planned outings with the children. I am continually inspired by the positive actions I see others taking to improve the community.

In 2000, the Department of Labor approved a job-related course in Professional Event Management at the George Washington University (GWU). It required a professional portfolio of lessons learned from the course. My portfolio showcased how I applied the skills learned to plan a fundraising event for NCBW and it was accepted for scholarly research in the GWU Gilman Library.

After major surgery in 2002 that resulted in five months of life support tube feeding, in 2003, I returned to college part-time determined to graduate. However, by 2005, I realized I needed an additional focus to keep motivated and prevent another interruption in my studies. Multi-tasking 

helps me stay focused and productive. I bought my dream car — a brand new silver S-Type Jaguar and I became a member of the **Order of the Eastern Star (OES).** In 2006 I became a member of the women's auxiliary to the **Ancient Egyptian Arabic Order of the Nobles of the Mystic Shrine**. Both organizations are part of the Prince Hall Masonic family and share traditions, values, and a commitment to charitable work and community service. 

To be a member of the Shriners, I had to be an OES member. My husband was a Mason. I attended many of his fundraising events. I was inspired to be a part of his charitable community service organization work.

OES and AEAONMS are international organizations that engage in a variety of activities centered on community service and philanthropy. These activities reflect their commitment to fostering leadership, community engagement, and support for various social causes. I served as an Event Planner for various fundraising events, including Gospel shows, prayer breakfasts, and scholarship fashion show luncheons. I selected venues, fashion coordinators, managed contract negotiations, designed floral decorations, and managed other event logistics. My most cherished achievement was serving as Mistress of Ceremony for the Women's Auxiliary to AEAONMS 100th Centennial Anniversary celebration, a moment that stands as a testament to my passion for community service. All events were successful, even while I was studying my college course work.

International Special Events Society (ISES) — In 2009, one of my professors at George Washington University asked me to volunteer to work on a special project where she was a member of the International Special Events Society, Washington, D.C. Chapter, and assist with decorating for their Awards Ceremony. As a team, I was tasked with the challenge of converting a mere party rental warehouse into an opulent banquet hall, I arranged china, flatware, glassware, chafing dishes, table linens, and other rental equipment to craft unique table centerpieces that would later be the talk of the town. This endeavor was not just about decoration; it was about creating an experience that would resonate with elegance and sophistication.

Illinois State Society Inaugural Gala Committee — 2009, the passion for my craft led me to volunteer with The Illinois State Society Inaugural Gala Committee for President Barack Obama. Here, I contributed to the decoration team that transformed the Washington, D.C. Renaissance Hotel meeting rooms into thematic designs that paid homage to historical Chicago landmarks and elements. Each opportunity was a canvas for creativity, and with every stroke of innovation, I found success.

Democratic National Committee Organizing for America —
On November 6, 2012, my dedication to civic engagement took me to
work with the Democratic National Committee Organizing for America in Germantown, Maryland. As part of the Phone Bank Project, I
reached out to potential supporters with a diplomatic touch, encouraging them to lend their voices in support of the re-election of President
Obama and his administration's plan.

The Democratic National Committee Organizing for America
project was not just a political endeavor; it was a challenge for my
communication skills, where every phone call was an opportunity to
practice empathy and persuasion. These experiences have not only
enriched my professional toolkit but have also shaped my character,
instilling in me a deeper sense of purpose and a commitment to
lifelong learning.

My time spent with the Democratic National Committee Organizing
for America was not only about supporting a political campaign; it was
about connecting with individuals from all walks of life and inspiring
them to be part of something bigger. The phone calls made may have
been brief, but the impact was lasting.

Presidential Inaugural Committee — My commitment to service continued with another special project. As I joined the ranks of
the 2013 Presidential Inaugural Committee in Washington, D.C. As
a 'VIP Concierge,' I had the honor of guiding guests and families of
President Barack Obama, Vice President Joe Biden, and esteemed
celebrities to their seats at the historic Lincoln Memorial during
President Obama's opening ceremony. It was a role that required
poise and precision, ensuring that every moment was seamless and
memorable.

I am filled with gratitude for the opportunities that have allowed
me to contribute to causes greater than myself. From the meticulous
artistry of transforming spaces into havens of celebration to guiding
dignitaries and celebrities, each role has been a thread in the fabric

of my journey. The laughter and camaraderie shared with fellow volunteers, the challenges overcome, and the successes achieved have all been invaluable lessons in leadership, empathy, and community.

Alpha Kappa Alpha Sorority, Inc.

On May 4, 2014, I was honored to be accepted into Alpha Kappa Alpha Sorority (AKA), Inc., Theta Omega Omega Chapter. AKA is a prestigious organization known for its commitment to community service. My journey with AKA has been a testament to

the power of collective effort and shared vision. As a proud member, I have had the honor of contributing to various committees, each with its unique purpose and impact.

From the Social Committee, where I found joy in assisting with the preparation of nourishing meals and creating welcoming spaces for our gatherings, to the Gulf Tournament Fundraising Committee, where I provided lovely floral decorations. My hands have crafted floral table centerpieces that not only adorned our events but also symbolized the beauty of our unity.

As the decorations chairperson for our chapter's forty-fifth and fiftieth anniversaries, I meticulously planned color schemes and production schedules, transforming ballrooms into celebratory havens that honored our rich history. The Father Daughter Dinner Dance Committee of 2019 entrusted me with creating a magical winter wonderland for young ladies to cherish and for the Debutant Cotillion Decorations Committee, I graced the tables and the room with elegant centerpieces and decorations to reflect the purpose of the event.

At the 2022 AKA North Atlantic Regional Conference (NARC), I participated in the NARC choir for both the opening and closing programs, as well as served on the decorations committee. One particular decoration project challenged me to transform several mannequins into dresses, using chair sashes, silk flowers and other ornaments. The decoration mannequins were strategically placed throughout the venue, and admired by all.  This experience taught me the importance of trying new things to discover hidden talents.

I take pride in my ability to create memorable experiences for attendees, ensuring that each event runs smoothly and achieves its goal. Each role I've embraced within these committees has been more than just a task; it has been a chapter in my story of growth, leadership, and service. They have shaped me into who I am today—a dedicated servant leader committed to making a difference in our community.

Reflecting on these experiences, I am grateful for the lessons learned and the friendships formed. Each event was an opportunity to serve and a moment to connect with others on a deeper level. The challenges we faced together strengthened our bonds and taught me the true meaning of resilience and teamwork. These memories are milestones and treasures that I carry with me as I continue to serve and inspire others.

To those embarking on their own journey of service and leadership, embrace every opportunity to contribute, learn from every challenge, and cherish every connection you make along the way. Be passionate about helping others and making a difference in the community.

I am struck by the profound personal growth that has blossomed from my volunteer experiences. Each event, each role, and each interaction has been a stepping-stone on my journey of self-discovery and development. The planning and execution of decoration projects have improved my organizational skills and attention to detail. Guiding VIPs and celebrities has taught me the art of diplomacy and grace under pressure. Collaborating with diverse teams has expanded my cultural awareness and adaptability.

These experiences have shaped my skills and instilled in me a profound sense of community. Volunteering has been my way of giving back, learning continuously, and making a difference — one event at a time.

Volunteering is more than just an act of kindness; it is a powerful way to connect with others and make a meaningful impact in our communities. Through volunteering, we not only provide support and resources to those in need but also foster a sense of unity and purpose. It allows us to share our skills, knowledge, and compassion, creating a ripple effect that can inspire others to contribute as well.

Also, volunteering enriches our own lives. It offers opportunities for personal growth, learning, and the development of new skills. It helps us build empathy and understanding, broadening our perspectives and deepening our appreciation for the diverse experiences of others. By giving our time and energy to causes we care about, we find a sense of fulfillment and joy that is truly unparalleled. Volunteering reminds us that we are all interconnected and that, together, we can create a better, more compassionate community.

On September 5, 2024, I transferred my AKA Theta Omega Omega Chapter membership to Zeta Omega Chapter to be closer to my residence. I am excited to find a place in my new chapter where I can continue to display my skills, follow my passion, and help others.

As I close this chapter of my memoir, I carry with me the invaluable lessons learned through service, the memories of each event, each person I met, and each moment that shaped me. Volunteering has been more than just an activity; it has been a way of life—a commitment to service, a dedication to excellence, and a passion for making a difference. In other words, it has become my hobby. My journey as a volunteer has been transformative, fostering resilience, compassion, and a relentless pursuit of excellence. It is my hope that my story will inspire others to take up the mantle of volunteerism and discover the joy and fulfillment that comes from giving back to their communities.

CHAPTER 6

ACCOLADES:
COMMENDATIONS AND AWARDS

Throughout my career, I have been fortunate to receive numerous commendations and awards that recognize my dedication, hard work, and contributions to public service.

In this chapter, I present a list of my most meaningful commendation letters and awards that mark significant milestones in my professional journey. Each accolade is a testament to the hard work and passion I poured into my profession. Each piece tells a story of perseverance, growth, and the impact of diverse experiences that have shaped my path from the fields of farm labor to the halls of the United States Department of Labor.

- **Department of Labor** — Distinguished Customer Service Medal for providing excellent customer service in advising congressional officials, attorneys, employers, and workers on the requirements of the WARN Act.

- **Department of Labor** — Letter for exceptional assistance to a Lawyer on a complex legal matter involving the WARN Act.

- **Department of Labor** — Special Act Award for moving a stalled Fallen Officers Grant Program that had Presidential support and involvement, and for developing the memorandum of understanding between the organizations to provide education and training to spouses of fallen police officers.

- **Department of Labor** — Letter for successfully coordinating logistical arrangements for several high-profile conferences within a short time frame.

- **Department of Labor** — Good Job Cash Award for creating well-written briefing papers and expert guidance on issues with proposed legislation to discuss with congressional staffers.

- **Department of Labor** — Letter for creating and delivering a first-rate implementation training package for the workforce system.

- **Department of Labor** — Gold Employee Service Award Pin for dedicated service.

- **George Washington University (GWU)** — Letter for creating one of the top 10 distinctive professional portfolios demonstrating the principles of event planning and management. The portfolios are used for scholarly research at the GWU Gelman Library.

- **White House/President Obama** — Retirement letter for dedication to Public Service.

- **Canaan Baptist Church** — Letter for providing furnishings and effectively decorating the church and the Hall of Faith Banquet Room.

- **AKA Theta Omega Omega Chapter** — Certificate of Appreciation for serving as Decorations Chairman providing outstanding performance, dedication and personal commitment to the successful execution of the 45th Anniversary Celebration and Awards Luncheon

- **AKA Theta Omega Omega Chapter, Ivy Vine Charities, Inc**. — Certificate of Appreciation for outstanding performance and lasting contribution to the 2019 Father Daughter Dinner Dance scholarship fund raising event.

These accolades are not just symbols of personal achievement but also reflections of the support and encouragement I have received from colleagues, mentors, and the communities I have served. I am deeply grateful to the many individuals who have supported me along the way. Their guidance, encouragement, and belief in my potential have been instrumental in my success.

ALL THINGS WORK TOGETHER FOR YOUR GOOD: *FROM VARIED ROLES TO EMPLOYMENT LAW EXCELLENCE*

This section, titled **"All Things Work Together for Your Good: From Varied Roles to Employment Law Excellence,"** is the essence of how my diverse job experiences shaped my role into a knowledgeable and empathetic WARN Act Policy/ Employment Law Advisor. Each role, a stepping-stone laid a foundation of deep understanding, empowering me to support workplace fairness with the insight of someone who has journeyed through many paths. My career, marked by hard work, perseverance, and faith, stands as proof that all of these experiences, however varied, come together to serve a greater purpose:

- **Agricultural Work** involves team work and communication. As a farm worker from the age of ten, I learned the value of hard work and dedication. The early mornings and long hours taught me the importance of perseverance and resilience. Working alongside a diverse team (my parents and older siblings), I developed strong communication skills and an appreciation for the fruits of labor. These experiences laid the groundwork for my future career, instilling in me a strong work ethic that has been invaluable in every job I've held since.

  Working on a farm requires a high level of coordination and cooperation. Each member of the team has a specific role, and success depends on everyone performing their tasks efficiently. I learned from watching and trusting my team and relying on their expertise, which taught me the importance of collaboration. This experience has been particularly beneficial in my later roles, where teamwork is crucial for achieving common goals.

  Clear communication is vital in agriculture, where safety and productivity are at stake. I had to learn to convey instructions clearly and listen actively. This not only improved my ability to work effectively with others but also enhanced my interpersonal skills. The ability to communicate effectively has been a cornerstone of my professional life, enabling me to build strong relationships with clients and colleagues.

These skills were instrumental in my career progression, allowing me to adapt to various work environments and take on leadership roles with confidence. The work ethic and teamwork developed on the farm was instrumental in my ability to collaborate with colleagues and contribute to team efforts in the government sector.

- **Retail Experience**: My time in retail was a significant period of growth, where I learned the intricacies of customer service and sales. Working in a fast-paced environment, I developed the ability to quickly adapt to changing situations and meet the needs of customers with diverse backgrounds. This role taught me the importance of patience, empathy, and problem-solving skills. I also gained a deep understanding of inventory management and the retail industry's dynamics, which have been beneficial in my subsequent roles.

My customer-centric approach from retail enhanced my interactions with the public and stakeholders, ensuring that their needs were met with efficiency and care.

In retail, every interaction with a customer is an opportunity to build a relationship and provide value. I learned to listen attentively to customer needs and preferences, which allowed me to offer personalized service and recommendations. This focus on the customer experience taught me the importance of going above and beyond to ensure satisfaction. It also highlighted the need for continuous learning about products and services to better serve customers.

This approach was a guiding principle in my career, influencing how I interact with clients and colleagues. It helped me to understand the importance of meeting and exceeding expectations, which is essential in any service-oriented role.

- **Hospitality Work:** The hospitality industry is all about creating memorable experiences for guests. My role in this sector taught me the importance of attention to detail and the ability to anticipate and meet the needs of others. I learned to manage high-pressure situations with grace and to maintain a positive attitude, even during challenging times. These skills have been invaluable in my career, as they have helped me to provide exceptional service and support in various professional settings.

  Hospitality also instilled in me a deep appreciation for cultural diversity and the importance of inclusivity. This has been particularly relevant in my work as a WARN Act Policy/Employment Law Advisor, where understanding and respecting different perspectives is crucial.

  The hospitality sector is dynamic and often unpredictable, requiring staff to be flexible and responsive to changing circumstances. I learned to quickly adjust to new situations, whether it was handling unexpected guest requests or managing last-minute changes in reservations. This environment taught me to think on my feet and find creative solutions to problems.

  Working with people from all walks of life enhanced my ability to adapt to different communication styles and cultural norms. This skill was particularly useful in my role as a WARN Act Policy/Employment Law Advisor, where I often interacted with a diverse range of clients and colleagues. The adaptability I gained from hospitality has been a cornerstone of my professional success, allowing me to thrive in various roles and industries.

As a **motel maid** in the hospitality industry, I was at the forefront of guest satisfaction. This role required meticulous attention to detail and a commitment to maintaining high standards of cleanliness and order. It also taught me the importance of time management and efficiency, as I had to balance multiple tasks while ensuring each room met the hotel's expectations.

As a **restaurant hostess/waitress** in the hospitality industry, I improved my customer service skills further. I learned the importance of meeting customer needs and maintaining a positive experience. I learned to navigate the fast-paced environment of a dining establishment, manage multiple tables, and provide prompt and courteous service. This role improved my ability to work under pressure and handle customer complaints with poise.

This customer-centric approach was vital in my advisory role, as I strived to understand and address the concerns of my customers effectively. Working in a restaurant taught me the value of collaboration and clear communication.

As a **caterer, floral designer, and decorator** in the hospitality industry, I showcased my creativity and organizational skills. I was responsible for bringing clients' visions to life, coordinating with vendors, and ensuring that events ran smoothly. This experience taught me the importance of teamwork and communication as I collaborated with various departments to deliver successful events.

These roles allowed me to express creativity and think outside the box. In my WARN Act Policy/Employment Law advisory role, this creativity helped me find innovative solutions to complex legal issues.

These experiences have not only shaped my professional capabilities but also my approach to problem-solving and client interaction, which made me a well-rounded and effective Employment Law Advisor.

The dynamic nature of the hospitality industry made me adept at adapting to new challenges. This adaptability is beneficial when navigating the ever-changing landscape of employment law.

The adaptability and attention to detail I learned and improved upon in hospitality allowed me to navigate the complexities of government work, where precision and flexibility were key.

Each of these roles contributed to my adaptability, attention to detail, and customer-centric approach, which were essential qualities in my role as a WARN Act Policy/ Employment Law Advisor.

- **Event Planning and Management:** My time as an event planner required a meticulous approach to ensure every detail was perfect. This attention to detail was crucial in my role as a WARN Act Policy/Employment Law Advisor, where I had to carefully review legal documents and regulations, and respond to telephone and written communications to provide accurate advice.

  Working in event planning also taught me the value of collaboration and clear communication. Event planning and management skills were essential when working with colleagues, clients, and other stakeholders in the legal field. My experience in event planning equipped me with organizational skills and the ability to manage multiple projects simultaneously, a valuable asset in any government role.

- **Community Service:** My involvement in the community service industry enriched my professional journey. Engaging in community service allowed me to connect with individuals from various backgrounds and understand their unique challenges. This experience fostered a deep sense of empathy and social responsibility, which were invaluable traits in my role as an Employment Law Advisor. I learned to advocate for those who may not have a voice, ensuring fair treatment and access to resources.

My time spent in community service improved my ability to listen and empathize with others. This skill was crucial when advising clients on WARN Act Employment Law issues, as it helped me to understand their perspectives and provide support that is both compassionate and practical.

Community service often requires finding creative solutions with limited resources. This resourcefulness translates well into my advisory role, where I had to navigate complex legal systems and find the best possible outcomes for my customers.

Taking on responsibilities in community service developed my leadership skills. As a WARN Act Policy/Employment Law Advisor, I drew upon this experience to lead initiatives, and guided others.

These aspects of my community service experience contributed to my personal growth and enhanced my professional capabilities, making me a more effective and compassionate WARN Act Policy/Employment Law Advisor. The empathy and advocacy skills made me a strong advocate for policies that benefit the public, reflecting a commitment to social responsibility.

These skills contributed to my success in the federal government and enabled me to approach challenges with a well-rounded perspective, making me an effective and respected Employment Law Advisor.

- **Clerical Office Work:** Starting in clerical roles, I developed a strong foundation in administrative tasks and organizational skills, which are essential for managing the complexities of the WARN Act Employment Law.

- **Secretary and Administrative Management Assistant:** These positions enhanced my ability to communicate effectively and manage information, skills that are crucial when advising on legal matters and developing compliance materials.

- **Workforce Development Specialist:** My experience in workforce development allowed me to understand the needs of workers and employers, providing valuable insights into the practical implications of the WARN Act Employment Law.

- **Employment Law Advisor:** As an advisor, I applied my comprehensive knowledge to analyze and explain the WARN Act. My ability to develop layoff compliance assistance material and advise various stakeholders showcased my expertise in this area.

Leading training and policy projects on the WARN Act Employment Law demonstrated my leadership skills and my commitment to ensuring that my team was well-informed and capable of implementing the law effectively.

Planning webinars and updating office procedures reflect my proactive approach to staying current with legal developments and ensuring that best practices were followed. All my diverse job experiences equipped me to advise others effectively.

My overall work experience taught me that the clerical and secretarial roles stand as pillars of organizational efficiency. Clerical work is the engine of office operations, requiring a meticulous eye for detail, proficiency in data entry, and a mastery of office technology. It calls for individuals who are adept at managing records, adept at navigating computer systems, and capable of multi-tasking in a busy environment.

The roles of clerical and secretarial work are often the unrecognized positions of career development. They are the foundational experiences that instill a diverse array of skills, which become invaluable in any professional path. The following is how these roles prepared me for other aspects of my career:

- **Organizational Skills:** Managing files, scheduling appointments, and coordinating events sharpened my ability to organize and prioritize tasks — a skill that is transferable to any job.

- **Communication:** Drafting correspondence, answering phones, and interacting with clients improved my verbal and written communication skills, making me an effective communicator.

- **Technical Proficiency:** Navigating various office software and equipment made me tech-savvy, a necessity in today's digital workplace.

- **Problem-Solving:** Handling unexpected issues and finding solutions quickly taught me to think critically and adapt to changing circumstances.

- **Attention to Detail:** The need for accuracy in clerical tasks ensured that I developed a keen eye for detail, which is crucial in avoiding mistakes and maintaining high-quality work.

- **Discretion:** Working with confidential information taught me the importance of discretion and integrity, traits that are highly valued in all levels of a career.

- **Time Management:** Meeting deadlines and managing a busy schedule trained me to work efficiently under pressure.

These roles likely served as a proving ground, where the skills and attributes I developed set the stage for my future successes, including my impactful work at the United States Department of Labor. They were not merely jobs but formative experiences that equipped me with a versatile toolkit for professional advancement and personal growth.

Starting a career in clerical work or secretarial positions is an exciting step that can open many doors. Here's some advice for those at the threshold of this journey:

- **Embrace Continuous Learning:** Stay curious and seek to expand your knowledge. Familiarize yourself with the latest office software and productivity tools, as these skills are often essential.

- **Improve Communication Skills:** Clear and effective communication is key. Practice both your written and verbal communication, as you'll be the liaison between different levels of the organization.

- **Develop Professionalism:** Maintain a high level of professionalism at all times. This includes punctuality, dress code, and a respectful demeanor.

- **Develop Organizational Abilities:** Strong organizational skills are the foundation of clerical and secretarial work. Create systems that help you stay organized and efficient.

- **Prioritize Time Management:** Learn to manage your time wisely. Balancing multiple tasks efficiently is crucial in these roles.

- **Be Adaptable:** The ability to adapt to new challenges and changing environments is invaluable. Be open to taking on new responsibilities as they arise.

- **Build Relationships:** Networking within your workplace can provide support and open up future career opportunities. Build positive relationships with your colleagues and superiors.

- **Protect Confidentiality:** You may be entrusted with sensitive information. It's imperative to maintain confidentiality and demonstrate your trustworthiness.

- **Seek Feedback:** Constructive feedback is a tool for growth. Welcome it, learn from it, and use it to improve your performance.

- **Show Initiative:** Don't be afraid to take the initiative and show your willingness to go beyond the job description. It's a great way to demonstrate your value to the organization.

My role was vital to the smooth operation of my office. With dedication and a willingness to learn and grow, I not only excelled in clerical or secretarial positions but also laid a strong foundation for my future career path.

My positions of clerical and secretarial roles instilled a work ethic and professional values that resonated throughout my career in these ways:

- **Precision and Accountability:** The meticulous nature of clerical tasks and the responsibility of managing sensitive information in secretarial work taught me the importance of accuracy and accountability in every undertaking task that I took.

- **Efficiency and Productivity:** These roles demand a high level of efficiency. I learned to optimize my workflow, manage time effectively, and prioritize tasks to meet deadlines and maintain productivity.

- **Integrity and Confidentiality:** Handling confidential documents and communications ingrained a deep sense of integrity and the need to uphold trust by safeguarding sensitive information.

- **Service Orientation:** Both positions require a service-oriented approach, whether supporting colleagues or managing client relations. This fostered a mindset of serving others diligently and with excellence.

- **Adaptability and Flexibility:** The dynamic nature of these jobs, with their varied tasks and challenges, taught me to be adaptable and flexible, ready to shift gears and tackle new challenges as they arise.

- **Professional Growth:** The exposure to different facets of the business world provided a broad perspective and understanding of organizational dynamics, contributing to my professional growth and readiness for future roles.

- **Leadership Qualities:** Especially in secretarial positions, I often had to take initiative, make decisions, and lead projects, which helped develop my leadership qualities. These roles laid the foundation for a strong work ethic and set of professional values that carried over into my subsequent career, including my impactful work at the United States Department of Labor. They shaped me into a professional who values precision, efficiency, integrity, service, adaptability, and continuous growth.

I would advise anyone beginning their journey in clerical or secretarial positions, that maintaining professionalism and a strong work ethic is paramount, as this is what helped me succeed in my career development:

- **Dress for Success:** Adhere to the dress code and present yourself neatly. Look the part. Your appearance sets the tone for how you're perceived and can impact your professional image.

- **Be Punctual:** Arriving on time, or even a few minutes early, shows respect for your colleagues' time and demonstrates reliability.

- **Stay Organized:** Keep your workspace tidy and your tasks well-managed. Organization is key to efficiency and helps in maintaining a professional demeanor.

- **Communicate Effectively:** Whether it's in writing or verbally, clear and professional communication is essential. Be mindful of your tone and the clarity of your messages.

- **Respect Confidentiality:** Treat all sensitive information with the utmost discretion. Trustworthiness is a cornerstone of professionalism.

- **Maintain a Positive Attitude:** A positive demeanor can improve the work environment for everyone. It also helps in dealing with stressful situations more effectively.

- **Demonstrate Initiative:** Show willingness to learn and take on new challenges. Being proactive can set you apart as a valuable team member.

- **Seek Continuous Improvement:** Be open to feedback and committed to personal and professional growth. Strive to be better each day.

- **Balance Assertiveness and Humility:** Stand up for your ideas and contributions when appropriate, but also be willing to admit mistakes and learn from them.

- **Cultivate Emotional Intelligence:** Develop the ability to read social cues and respond appropriately. Emotional intelligence is crucial in navigating workplace dynamics.

My early experiences in these roles were building blocks for my career. I made some mistakes, but I learned from them. By upholding a strong work ethic and professionalism from the start, I laid a solid foundation for future success and advancement.

CHAPTER 8

RETIREMENT: EMBRACING THE GOLDEN YEARS

s I reflect on the journey that has led me to this moment of retirement, I am filled with a profound sense of gratitude and accomplishment. On January 31, 2014, I bid farewell to my public service role as a GS-13 WARN Act Policy/Employment Law Advisor at the United States Department of Labor, a chapter that was both challenging and rewarding.

I found my true calling as an Employment Law Advisor for the WARN Act. My role involved helping workers, employers, lawyers, and other public interest groups understand the intricacies of the law. But it was the workers, often overwhelmed and confused, who needed the most patience and support.

Serving as an Employment Law Advisor gave me many opportunities to make a real difference in people's lives. I remember countless instances where I went beyond merely explaining the law. When workers needed assistance with matters outside my purview, I didn't just hand them a phone number. I made the calls for them, leveraging my position to get the answers they needed.

The most impactful and memorable moment of my role is when one day, I received a call from a gentleman who said he did not have a WARN Act question and had heard that I was "someone who helped people." That moment touched me deeply. It was a testament to the impact of my extra efforts and reinforced my belief in the importance of going the extra mile. My role as an Employment Law Advisor aligned with my passion for helping others in need. Overall, my career was a tapestry woven from diverse threads—each job contributed to my experience.

When I retired, I did not want the same typical going away party and speeches that everyone gets, so I left quietly. As usual, I completed all my work assignments on time and I sent an e-mail to my supervisors and colleagues, and simply said, "Effective Immediately, I am retired." I explained where all completed projects and files were located, and walked swiftly out my office door. I was satisfied just knowing that I provided excellent customer service, made a positive difference, and contributed to the success and mission of the United States Department of Labor, Employment and Training Administration, Office of Rapid Response.

In June 2014, I received a retirement letter from President Barrack Obama. His recognition letter meant more to me than any celebration. Besides, I really did not want to say good-bye, as it makes me very emotional. Retirement brings a sense of loss for such fulfilling experiences. However, I believe the knowledge and skills I've gained throughout my career will continue to serve me well, whether in retirement or in any endeavors that I may pursue.

Now, I embrace the golden years with my husband, living in a big beautiful three car garage home — a far cry from what I grew up in. I find joy in the simplicity and fulfillment of my retirement life. My hobbies and interests paint a true picture of a vibrant and active lifestyle, filled with travel, cultural enrichment and personal growth. From the grandeur of Broadway shows to the grace of ballet and ice skating performances, each experience has been a celebration of the arts. My love for music extends to singing, where I find joy in harmonizing with my church choir, and to decorating, where I channel my creativity into floral designs that bring beauty to any space. Joining a line dancing club and the Red Hat Society ladies social club have been some of the highlights of my retirement, offering exercise, fun, camaraderie, and a way to stay connected with people who share my passions.

My Sundays are devoted to service to my church, where I serve as a choir member, and upon request provide decorating assistance. One of my most cherished church projects is when I was honored to have the opportunity to transform our new Hall of Faith building into a space of beauty and reverence. The Hall of Faith building is a significant project that stands as a symbol of spiritual growth and community within our church. The hall was designed to be a welcoming space for all members, reflecting the values and beliefs that we hold dear.

In selecting the color scheme, the idea was for a color that would suggest a sense of peace and serenity, with warm tones that invite reflection and contemplation. The flooring materials were chosen for their durability and ease of maintenance, ensuring that the space would remain pristine for years to come.

Furniture and wall art were carefully chosen to complement the overall artistic nature of the hall, with each piece contributing to a cohesive and harmonious environment. Window treatments were selected to allow natural light to filter in, creating an ambiance that is both bright and comforting. The artifacts arranged throughout the hall were not just decorative elements; they were chosen to tell a story — a story of faith, perseverance, and community.

The tireless efforts put into decorating the Hall of Faith have been met with great appreciation from church members and my Pastor, who expressed his gratitude through a heartfelt thank you letter. It is a testament to the power of dedication.

When I started this project, I was not sure what to do. I prayed for direction, as I believe in Proverbs 3:5-6 (KJV), "Trust in the Lord with all thy heart and lean not to thine own understanding. In all thy ways acknowledge Him and He shall direct thy paths." To God be the glory for the things He has done for me. His grace and mercy brought me through.

As I continue to work in my church and charitable organizations, I am reminded of the joy that comes from using my skills to serve others. The Hall of Faith project was a chance to challenge myself creatively. Without formal training, I relied on my intuition and the inspiration drawn from luxury magazines and model homes. It was a journey of self-discovery, where I learned to trust my vision and the guidance of my faith.

I also use my retirement time to decorate my home. It has become a showcase of tasteful design, so much so that it caught the eye of Toll Brothers luxury home builders' managers and sales representative who were impressed enough to compensate me to feature it as a model for several potential buyers.

In retirement, I continue to use my knowledge and skills to help others, embodying the spirit of Philippians 2:4 (NKJV) that says, "… Let each of you look out not only for his own interests, but also for the interests of others." It is in giving that I have found my true pleasure and purpose. My passion for helping others is beautifully captured in the words of Mahalia Jackson's song: "If I can help somebody, my living shall not be in vain." In my experience of helping somebody, I learned that I can only help those who really want to be helped. Some have wasted my time. After I provide them help, they do nothing with it. On the other hand, it is rewarding to know they appreciate my help when they do. I tell my story as Matthew 5:16 (KJV) advises, "Let your light so shine before men that they may see your good works…" My journey has been a long and winding road, but it ultimately guided me in the right direction.

As I look back on my life's work and forward to the days ahead, I am reminded that every experience has been a stepping-stone to this point — a point where I can say with confidence that I have evolved.

Husband and me cruising and enjoying retirement life together.

"We travel not to escape life, but for life not to escape us."

CHAPTER 9

THE BUTTERFLY EFFECT: *A SUMMARY OF MY TRANSFORMATION*

My work life journey began in the fields of farm labor, where I learned strong work ethics, and the value of hard work and perseverance. From those early days, I carried with me a determination to rise above my circumstances and pursue a career that would allow me to make a meaningful impact. This memoir is a reflection on the journey that has shaped me, the challenges I've overcome, and the dreams I've pursued.

As I transitioned into various roles, each step was marked by a commitment to excellence and a passion for continuous learning. My dedication did not go unnoticed, leading to opportunities that allowed me to contribute significantly to my field of work.

Throughout my life, I have embraced the journey of continuous learning and growth, starting from the humble beginnings of a farm worker at the tender age of ten. Each role I've undertaken, from the farm fields to the halls of the U.S. Department of Labor, has been a stepping stone in my career. The agricultural sector taught me the value of hard work and perseverance; retail enhanced my customer service and sales skills; hospitality instilled in me the importance of hospitality and attention to detail; entertainment sparked my creativity and adaptability; community service deepened my understanding of social issues and empathy; and my tenure in federal government provided me with a comprehensive understanding of employment law and policy. These varied experiences have not only shaped my professional expertise but have also molded me into a well-rounded individual, prepared to contribute meaningfully to any endeavor I undertake.

One of my proudest achievements was my tenure at the United States Department of Labor, where I had the privilege of serving in a capacity that aligned with my values and expertise. My contributions during this time were instrumental in shaping policies and initiatives that supported workers across the nation.

Throughout my journey, I have improved a diverse set of skills, from leadership and strategic planning to effective communication and problem-solving. These skills have not only propelled my career but have also enabled me to mentor others and foster a culture of growth within my teams.

Looking back on my path from farm labor to a role at such a prestigious department, I am reminded of the power of resilience and the importance of seizing opportunities for growth. Driven by a desire to serve and uplift others, I ventured beyond the fields to pursue higher education. It was a path fraught with obstacles, but each step forward was a step closer to my purpose. My journey through academia was not just about gaining knowledge; it was about discovering my place in the world.

The pursuit of education was not without its trials. Balancing work and study required discipline and sacrifice, but it also brought clarity and focus. Each challenge overcame was a step closer to my purpose, each lesson learned a building block for my future. It was during this time that I discovered my passion for public service. The principles I had learned on the farm — hard work, community, and resilience — found new expression in my studies. I realized that my journey was not just about personal growth but about contributing to something greater than myself.

I have chronicled my transformative journey through various volunteer experiences that have shaped my life and character. From orchestrating grand events to guiding dignitaries, each chapter has been a testament to the power of service and community. The challenges faced and overcome have not only enhanced my skills but also deepened my understanding of leadership, empathy, and resilience.

As I reflect on these experiences, I am reminded of the personal growth that has blossomed from each endeavor. The meticulous planning, the diplomatic engagements, and the collaborative efforts have all contributed to a richer, more fulfilling life. This memoir is not just a record of events; it is a celebration of the human spirit's capacity for kindness, learning, and making a positive difference.

Just as a caterpillar transforms into a butterfly, my life has undergone its own metamorphosis. The mistakes I made throughout my career and challenges I faced have become the wings that carry me forward, and the lessons I've learned are the colors that adorn my flight. I invite readers to join me in this reflection, to see themselves in my story, and to be inspired to embark on their own journeys of discovery and service and find their wings.

As the sun sets on the fields that raised me, I stand tall at the helm of change, knowing that every seed sown in determination has blossomed into a legacy of progress — this is not just my work life journey it is the path of *Evolved: From the Fields of Farm Labor to the United States Department of Labor.*

www.ingramcontent.com/pod-product-compliance
Lightning Source LLC
Chambersburg PA
CBHW040759150726
48196CB00040B/916/J